This workbook belongs to _____

_____

This workbook is a companion to *Boost Core Power and Bust Anxiety.* Here are things said about that book that this workbook builds upon:

"The idea of making friends with anxieties is very freeing...intellectually helpful!" –BW, Professional Pianist

"Loved! My hypothesis was this would be helpful for high-level competitors. True, but more! It also applies to regular, routine life. Incredibly empowering. A book for the masses." –ML, three time 1st Place Dance Collegiate National Champion, 1st Place International Title, Choreographer

"I was asked to review this book while adding certification to my helicopter pilot license. I didn't think I had time. Reading saved me time! The info cut down study time for the exam and expensive flight time learning maneuvers. Highly recommend." –CR, Commercial Helicopter Pilot

"Good insight into body and brain functions under stressful situations and how to navigate the brain through barriers in daily life. Very insightful." –CH, Education Administrator

"Valuable reinforcement! Recognizing patterns that drag down energy and performance is valuable not just to players but also coaches and parents." –SD, Sports Team Manager, Parent of Cal Ripkin World Series athlete

"This book changed how I look at and empower myself. The questions and case studies were helpful in analyzing a deeper look. It's too good to skim!" –PH, Business Banker

"I definitely needed to read this! I realized most of my stress comes from outcome anxiety. I learned awesome skills that I hope will also help my children." –SM, Student, Parent

"Finding fear is a friend was a tad insightful. I never considered overcoming anxiety a whole-body approach. Short, sweet chapters engage personal connections. Oh that all can have this confidence, especially worried teens!" –MM, Teacher, Musician, Parent of champion athletes

"What an amazing book! I found it to be engaging, insightful, practical, universally applicable, and full of life-changing concepts. I do not know a single person who would not benefit. Well done."–KB, Top 1% Scholar

CORE POWER
PRO–LAUNCH PAD

VIP Companion Workbook to
Boost Core Power and Bust Anxiety
How to Overcome Outcome Anxiety like Performance, Test, Sports, Public Speaking, Appearance,
Technology, Stage, Finance, Business, or Relationship Anxiety for PEAK Ability

By Mariann R. Adams, MS, NCTM

To give feedback, receive private coaching
See other books by Mariann R. Adams
Schedule a lecture, enjoy tips, or
Other information see:
www.aplusperformingarts.com

Illustrations: Kamryn Brockbank
Photo: Teresa Lynn Anderson

Adams, Mariann R.
The Core POWER Pro-Launch Pad: VIP workbook to Boost Core Power and Bust Anxiety
ISBN-13: 978-1-7326959-1-7
ISBN-10: 1-7326959-1-1
1. Performance, Test, Sports Anxiety—psychological, neurological, physiological
2. Stress management
3. Self help techniques

To
Bart, Ara, and Jim
Sherie, Brian, Karen, Julie, JJ, and Michelle

Introduction
Build Core Power

You are the VIP detective for yourself to remove the *causes* of anxiety. You are also the VIP security officer for yourself to prevent anxiety. No one can do these jobs for you. This book is designed to help you carry out these jobs so that your core is strong and safe.

You are unique. Your experiences are unique. Your genes are unique. Your personality is unique. If you have anxiety, your anxiety is unique. (If you don't have anxiety, the things that prevent anxiety will be unique). This workbook is a companion to *Boost Core Power and Bust Anxiety.* It is designed to maximize the benefits of that book. It applies book concepts to your unique situation to decrease anxiety and increase ability. A strong, safe core automatically dissipates anxiety and increases brain and body function.

This workbook has two sections:
I. **Increase Understanding**—building core strength through a thorough understanding of core concepts.

II. **Increase Ability**—building core ability through directed observations during daily life, practice, or performance.

This workbook is designed to build core power. It assists individuals in proactively overcoming anxiety or proactively preventing it. Anxiety management skills are beneficial for any person since everyone "performs" daily. Additionally, there is a constant bombardment of influences that exploit and increase anxiety—from appearance anxiety to information overload. This workbook is used by individuals and universities to assist in eliminating anxiety and enhancing ability. Individuals or institutions aspiring to stand out in academics, sports, the performing arts, or business must also stand out in anxiety management. High performance and anxiety management are inseparable. Anxiety is an important issue. It presents an occupational hazard with serious long-term health ramifications. A thorough understanding of it develops emotional IQ which is repeatedly shown as the greatest single factor for success. This workbook is designed to build core power and provide that emotional IQ edge.

Note to teachers: Section I (Chapters 1-28) and Section II (Propel Progress A) can be done simultaneously. Quarter classes do approximately three of the short book/workbook chapters/week; semester classes do about two chapters/week. Section II begins 3-4 weeks after Section I to establish an initial base of understanding. Power point and additional teaching materials available with proof of teacher and institute status. Questions/comments see aplusperformingarts.com or info@aplusperforming arts.com.

Table of Contents

Introduction

Section I.
Increase Understanding

Building core strength through a
Thorough understanding of core concepts.

This section builds core strength through a thorough understanding of core concepts. It consists of twenty-eight chapters. Each chapter contains both review and new material, space to write observations and these sections:

Empower Yourself
> To encapsulate core power concepts

Chapter Summary Bullet Points
> To review and increase core power comprehension

Case Studies
> To clarify core power concepts

ReflACTION Questions
> To apply core power skills

Journal Insights
> To enhance personal core power processing

Test Yourself
> To increase awareness of important concepts

1

1. Rickety Bridges
Understanding

Empower Yourself
Rickety, or...reliable.

Summary
- There are huge benefits in understanding anxiety.
- Eliminating fear starts with understanding core safety. Fear never happens without core safety concerns.
- Brains and bodies are hard-wired for safety. Physical safety is usually guarded, emotional safety isn't.
- Safety concerns draw attention from other things, safety affects ability. There are real threats when performing.
- Outcome Anxiety is any anxiety where there's a fear of not coming out okay. Everyone has outcome anxiety at times.
- A performance is anytime ability is demonstrated.
- Peak flow in the zone is top, pleasurable ability.
- Incapacitating anxiety and fleeting inconsistency are degrees of the same thing.

- Fear dissipates when the core is strong. It's almost impossible to override fear responses; it's relatively easy to build core power.
- One-size-fits-all strategies don't work because each person's anxiety is unique. The only way to eliminate anxiety is to meet core needs.
- Anxiety info is important for leaders and parents.
- Anxiety info is curative, preventative, and collaborative; it improves individual and group performance.

Case Study

Brett enjoyed coaching, but was frustrated when players seemed stuck in a slump. He had no idea that anxiety was such a factor until he understood strategies to overcome it. He structured his team practices to include beneficial things to reduce anxiety and strengthen the core power of his players. This helped him maximize talent despite the variety of personalities and abilities on his team.

Case Study

Chad was out-going and figured he could get along with just about anyone until lately at work. He didn't know how to approach a growing problem. He thought that by "forgiving and forgetting" things would resolve, but a co-worker was clearly taking advantage of him. It was a relief to recognize that the uncomfortable feelings were anxiety and that it was appropriate for him to protect his core. It was also helpful to know that he could protect others while protecting himself by giving and expecting respect as problems were addressed. [It is common for people to struggle with both guilt and blame when the core is not adequately protected. Proactively protecting the core is good for both sides of any situation.]

Case Study

When York first learned of anxiety prevention he thought it didn't apply to him. But as he learned more he realized that the uncomfortable feelings he felt as he met with prospective clients were a form of anxiety—maybe he wasn't on stage or playing a sport, but his work was a type of performance, nevertheless. He also realized that his CE exams measured his performance. It was useful to know how to manage anxiety and come out on top in both situations.

Fast Track ReflACTION

1) Describe a situation in which hard-wired automatic defense mechanisms kicked in to protect you physically this week.

_____

_____

_____

2) Name a situation this week in which you were unsure how to manage a situation.

_____

_____

_____

3) Describe a time you tried to override automatic fear responses; what possible core issues were not met?

_____

_____

_____

Journal Insights

Write insights regarding the chapter contents. Insights might include how these concepts affect you: "unsure-of-coming-out-okay" situations you experience, physical and emotional safety, achieving peak flow in the zone through increased core strength, anxiety information as preventative.

_____

_____

_____

_____

_____

_____

_____

Test Yourself

   A. Name three commonly recognized anxieties mentioned in this chapter.

   _____

   _____

   B. Name three types of anxieties mentioned in this chapter that are rarely acknowledged as anxiety.

   _____

   _____

   C. What two things have the same root cause but are at opposite ends of the spectrum? What is the common root?

   _____

   _____

   D. Name three things that are "performances" but are not generally recognized as such.

   _____

   _____

   E. Name three possible real threats from performing.

   _____

   _____

2. Measly Monsters
Discerning

Empower Yourself
Dodge problems, or…determine solutions.

Summary

- To eliminate anxiety, focus must shift from managing symptoms to eliminating causes.
- Discouragement is the result of working on the wrong thing.
- Problems are usually due to the method not the person.
- The idea is to eliminate problems, not learn to cope with them.
- You have a unique VIP history, so the specific things that eliminate your anxiety will also be unique.
- Efforts must be focused in the right direction to be effective.
- To eliminate anxiety and strengthen the core, an individual's unique personality and background must be considered.
- Insight comes through conscious and subconscious processing.
- Honest, curious reflection speeds processing.
- Problems dissipate when thoroughly understood.

- Solutions are usually different than realized or problems would already be solved.
- Little things make a difference.

Case Study

Suzie thought there was a monster under her bed. When her mother helped her look under the bed and out the window (instead of coping with the "monster" by breathing deeply, systematically relaxing, focusing on senses, reframing, avoiding catastrophic thoughts, etc.) her core was strengthened and the fear automatically melted. When the causes of fear are understood and addressed, core safety is restored and fear automatically dissipates.

Case Study

Brent's love of the game decreased as the pressure increased. If not for his scholarship he would have quit already. He felt like a fraud, despite solid stats and interested scouts. He churned inside and hid the problem. Then, in a special interview, a respected pro player admitted to having performance anxiety and explained how he dealt with it. This was a ray of hope. Brent was determined to figure this problem out. He actually loved the sport; it was the anxiety he hated.

Case Study

Aileen came out of the anxiety seminar more frustrated than ever. She had already tried *every* technique presented by this anxiety expert! Sure they helped but they were time consuming and unpredictable in their results. She felt like she was on a roller-coaster, never feeling like anything was reliable. Was it possible to get rid of this problem or did she have to live with it forever?

Fast Track ReflACTION

1) How does anxiety affect your ability (or those you mentor)? What could be gained by performing better? Do you ever hide or suppress anxiety?

_____

_____

_____

2) Do you experience any of these outcome anxieties: inconsistency, frustrations, agitation, insecurity, dread, avoidance, irritability, procrastination, or apprehension; how could addressing anxiety improve relationships and health?

_____

_____

_____

3) In the past, if anxiety has surfaced have you addressed *causes*, targeted *symptoms*, simply *ignored,* or *avoided* situations? What was the result? What insights have surfaced and how do they affect your perspective, motivation and hope?

_____

_____

_____

Journal Insights

Write insights regarding the chapter contents. Insights might include how these concepts affect you: managing symptoms vs. eliminating causes, working on the right thing, discouragement or avoidance, the concept of fear dissipating when core safety issues are thoroughly understood and addressed.

_____

_____

_____

_____

_____

_____

_____

_____

Test Yourself

    A. Name three common ways of addressing anxiety *symptoms*.

_____

_____

    B. Susie's fear automatically dissipated when what?

_____

_____

    C. What must be realized to prevent being put off and missing "anxiety busting gems"?

_____

_____

    D. No matter how sincere Suzie is, name three things that could happen if she addresses symptoms instead of causes?

_____

_____

    E. How long did it take for Suzie's fear to disappear in the second scenario; if you experience anxiety why is the solution probably different than you think?

_____

_____

3. Ready, Set—Unlearn
Reflecting

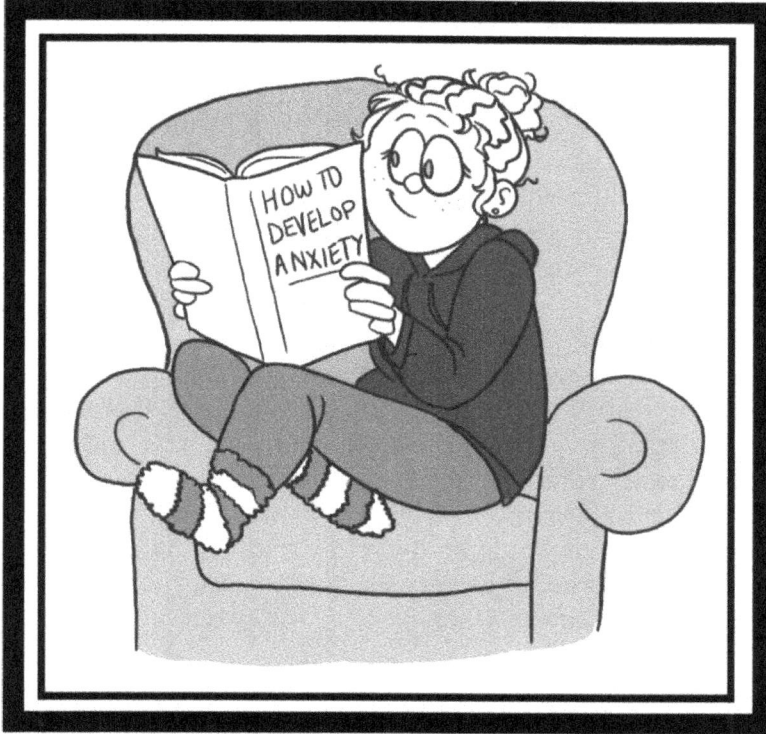

Empower Yourself
Take a detour, or...get to the core.

Summary

- There are benefits to understanding outcome anxiety whether a person is strutting or struggling.
- Outcome anxiety is common, those who *don't* have it are the odd ones.
- Anxiety is hidden due to embarrassment, fear, or discouragement.
- Thinking others manage better increases anxiety.
- Everyone has hard stuff and easy stuff, anxiety is the hard stuff for some.
- Anxieties are learned and can be "unlearned."
- Young children don't have outcome anxiety.
- Anxiety develops from experiences, observations, imprinting, genes, and personality.
- Most people have hang-ups and "pigeon-hole".
- Identifying past contributing factors speeds progress in eliminating anxiety; being stuck in the past, blame and guilt slow progress.

- Limitations may be uncontrollable but they don't determine success.
- Limitations are not handicaps; they're opportunities with benefits.
- Limitations can strengthen the core.
- Moving forward is facilitated by knowledge.

Case Study

Abam felt he wasn't good at technology. This limited his ability to share his areas of expertise. After he learned about imprinting, Abam reconsidered his abilities. Whenever frustrated, he asked himself, "Why am I unsure? What about this is too hard for me? Why do I feel incapable of handling this situation?" It seemed a mental door widened enabling him to learn things he had struggled with. He was better at technology than he thought. [As you'll see later, brain function literally changes when there's anxiety and then these types of questions are asked.]

Case Study

Bork looked confident and strong but there was a part of him that was angry at his dad for the alcoholism that left their family shattered. He blamed his dad for his lingering fear of confronting difficult situations. One day Bork took a different look. The years of anger had gotten him nowhere. He was backed against the wall and ready to try something new. He had never considered that he didn't have to have a perfect past to move on. Maybe he just had to acknowledge that it was what it was and that he would no longer be defined by it. He didn't know if this perspective would work, but he decided to try. It was like a weight lifted. He did move forward as he accepted where he was, realized he didn't h have to make everything right in one day, and that he could grow.

Case Study

Karen watched her children swim as they demanded her attention—and everyone else in the pool it seemed! Was she ever that way? Her mother told stories of her antics and lack of inhibition. She wondered if the spontaneous fun-loving part of her was gone forever. As she thought she questioned, "Why not find it!" She took off the towel hiding her less than perfect figure and jumped in. She had admired those who seemed unconcerned about what they looked like and just had fun. Why couldn't she be one of those people?

Fast Track ReflACTION
1) What possible limitations do you sense within; what may have caused them?

_____

_____

_____

2) What factors determine whether limitations propel or hamper? What can you do to ensure benefits from any limitations you experience?

_____

_____

_____

3) What is easy for you; how can you use these strengths to overcome limitations?

_____

_____

_____

Journal Insights

Write insights regarding the chapter contents. Insights might include how these concepts affect you: strengths and weaknesses, reactions to limitations, how you perceive you manage in relation to others, where limitations originated.

_____

_____

_____

_____

_____

_____

_____

Test Yourself

A. Name three of the four things that anxiety develops from.

_____

_____

B. Name five possible beneficial qualities that may develop from having a limitation.

_____

_____

C. Deep, awesome _____ is the most powerful weapon to eliminate_____ and increase _____.

_____

_____

D. In the past, what can leave pockets of anxiety and negatively impact here and there?

_____

_____

E. Who benefits, and how far can these benefits reach, if you address anxiety?

_____

_____

4. Performance Anxiety Doesn't Exist
Recognizing

Empower Yourself
Disconnected core, or…distinguished core.

Summary
- Most names for anxiety are "outcome anxiety" or feeling unsure of coming out okay. The mind and body react to feeling unsure.
- Names define problems. An accurate name provides direction. An inaccurate name limits progress and can result in discouragement.
- There's greater fear of not coming out okay when there's an audience. Fear immediately causes limitations in practice and performance.
- Usually unsure feelings are a symptom of primary fears like feeling loved, accepted, appreciated, secure, valued, and capable.
- Everyone experiences primary needs and fears at times.
- Even if a performance bombs, a person will be okay if feeling loved, good enough, understood, accepted, appreciated, important, capable, or valued. Conversely, even when a performance shines, a person will not be okay if not feeling loved, good enough, understood, accepted, appreciated,

important, capable, or valued. Unsure feelings are compounded by being unsure of support.

- "Unlovable" things tend to be hidden from self and others. Optimally, supportive people are both kind and knowledgeable. Disconnection clogs subconscious and conscious problem solving and impedes confidence. Disclosure is not always wise. Connection to one's core is always wise.
- Stress is an occupational hazard for performers. Stress has serious physical, mental, and interpersonal consequences. The skills that decrease anxiety also reduce stress.
- Skills improve enjoyment, relationships, learning rates, stamina, health, and performance ability.

Case Study

Terrie churned inside. She decided to leave the exhibition hall and pace in the lobby until her turn. As she prepared to exit, her friend, Midgett, gently teased, "Relax! There's no need for performance anxiety." Terrie felt defensive. This was just extra energy, and certainly to be expected! After all, she couldn't be sure she would handle everything well until she was done. Peeved, she snapped, "Seriously! I just want to walk. I'm *fine*!" Midgett knew that anxiety could change personalities and responded, "Good idea. I'll come for you a couple of minutes before. You'll do great." [Terrie disconnected from herself and others by not understanding or acknowledging anxiety and not being aware.]

Case Study

Bill slammed shut the book and walked away. His brain was fried. He didn't see how he could ever be ready for the test. He did awful on the practice test yesterday and today studying seemed even harder. He wished he hadn't taken the practice test. He couldn't imagine 6 more weeks in this prep class. Would it even matter? But how could he face his friends and family if he didn't try; then again, how could he face them if he did? [Bill's mind and body are reacting to anxiety, making it difficult to prepare. His anxiety is due to being "unsure of coming out okay" and is made worse by concerns regarding primary needs.]

Case Study

Leslie sheepishly returned to the bench. Her coach teased, "Well that wasn't your best job!" She winked and put an arm on Leslie's shoulder. Still embarrassment tugged at Leslie. Her coach noticed and continued, "Don't be too worried about it, some days are just off. You're a solid performer and everyone is entitled to a down day now and then. Let me go over my observations with you so you can choose your next performance goal." Leslie shrugged the embarrassment off and refocused as her coach gave a reassuring smile and shared her notes.

Fast Track ReflACTION

1) How does the name "outcome anxiety" affect anxiety-elimination tactics? How could having anxiety when in practice or alone impact a performance?

_____

_____

_____

2) What primary fears speak more strongly to you; why? (Consider the impact of nature/nurture.)

_____

_____

_____

3) What unlovable things do you hide from yourself or others? What are the advantages and disadvantages of hiding things? How can you use awareness to better support yourself?

_____

_____

_____

Journal Insights

Write insights regarding the chapter contents. Insights might include how these concepts affect you: types of anxiety hampering you, disconnection from self or others, feelings about primary needs.

_____

_____

_____

_____

_____

_____

_____

Test Yourself
    A. Why does more fear surface in performance?

_____

_____

    B. What are the two names of outcome anxiety that can happen _after_ a performance?

_____

_____

    C. What two things are needed for true confidence rather than positive fluff?

_____

_____

    D. Name the primary occupational hazard for performers and what are the effects of it?

_____

_____

    E. The skills that decrease anxiety also increase_____ and reduce _____ and improve _____.

_____

_____

5. The Inseparables
Connecting

Empower Yourself
Insufficient preparation, or…invincible preparation.

Summary
- Performance and anxiety management are inseparable.
- Performance preparation should include anxiety management.
- Anxiety management can be practiced with skill development, but it doesn't happen automatically.
- Preparation strategies are different when eliminating anxiety. Lack of awareness can result in difficulty moving forward.
- Awareness does not mean to become bogged down or distracted.
- Awareness involves being mindful and curious.
- Thoughts and feelings during practice bond with the skill and affect performance. Unsure feelings can be fleeting or overwhelming.
- Unsure feelings can be directly, indirectly, or unrelated to performance.
- You are the only person with access to your thoughts and feelings, so you are the only one who can collect your data.
- There are always reasons for unsure feelings, and the subconscious and conscious brain is able to uncover them.
- Awareness puts the subconscious brain on scan mode and the conscious brain on reception mode.
- Anxiety management is straightforward.

Case Study

Klon was overwhelmed. How could he succeed when his college classes were filled with smart students who came from neighborhoods that were night-and-day different from his own gang-and-drug-filled one? Self-doubt grew and rattled him as a big test neared. It was the first he'd really become aware of his feelings. He confided his concerns to his roommate, TJ, who responded, "Look, if you don't deserve to be here, nobody deserves to be here. Just because no one at home has done this doesn't mean you can't. You made it this far, who says you can't take it all the way?" Klon's doubts subsided enough that he was able to work again. He studied fiercely and aced the test.

Case Study

Not again! Performance was just like practice…mistakes, mistakes, mistakes…Leigh questioned himself. He would ever get it right! He was just a failure. It seemed like this happened no matter what he did. Why try? Everyone said this happened to his dad, too. Maybe they were both just born losers. [This case study is typical of how many people feel, but it is so negative it should be immediately countered. It's likely that Leigh has genetic, nature, and nurture factors affecting ability. However, while these indirect factors may influence his situation, as Leigh understands anxiety he can rise above the past and shape the future. He is not doomed, as you will see.]

Case Study

The music vibrated throughout the empty hall. This evening would be great! Dave felt absolutely ready for tonight. Rehearsal went well except the first couple of measures. He felt a little nervous in those, but it was probably okay. It was likely that he was just warming up to the room. [Note: while the problem might stem from not being warmed up, Dave should probably double check. The things that are a little unsure in practice are often the things that cause problems in performance. Attention to unsure feelings can make all the difference.]

Fast Track ReflACTION

1) What might have happened if Klon above *didn't* explore unsure feelings; what if Terrie in the last chapter *did* explore unsure feelings?

_____

_____

_____

2) How can you improve the quality of thoughts and feelings during study or practice; what could be the impact beyond improved performance?

_____

_____

_____

3) How does noticing unsure feelings increase the ability to trust and support yourself, accept support from others, and give support to others?

_____

_____

_____

Journal Insights

Write insights regarding the chapter contents. Insights might include how these concepts affect you: past efforts to prepare anxiety management, quality of thoughts and feelings during specific tasks, impact on flow/zone or anxiety, direct/indirect/unrelated performance factors, unsure feelings affecting you.

_____

_____

_____

_____

_____

_____

_____

Test Yourself

A. Ignoring anxiety is common. Name the three reasons why anxiety management is neglected?

_____

_____

B. Practice is a time to improve what two inseparable things?

_____

_____

C. _____ isn't a big deal; but they provide valuable ____ _____ and that's a _____ _____.

_____

_____

D. Unsure feelings can be _____ _____ _____ related to performance; like a ball grip.

_____

_____

E. Anxiety is fluid. Performance ability can increase or decrease from emotional things like _____ _____; what wasn't a problem can become one and what was a problem may dissipate. So continual _____ is needed.

_____

_____

6. Fear is Your Friend
Embracing

Empower Yourself
Ignore symptoms, or…identify symptoms.

Summary
- Edgy fear prepares you to succeed.
- Adrenalin enhances ability, sharpens thinking, and strengthens muscles.
- Fear can be a good friend in personal life, practice or performance.
- Edgy and over-edgy fear produces physical, mental, emotional, and behavioral symptoms.
- Some fear is common, other fear is uncommon and often unrecognized.
- It's important to be able to spot all fear.
- Maximum ability starts inside.
- It's unlikely to have all fear symptoms, or no symptoms.

- Fear is unique to the individual.
- Fear changes behavior and personalities, and these changes are often seen right before a performance. There can be bonding or conflict.
- Fear can cause a person to over-engage or under-engage.
- Taking a few minutes to address anxiety saves time. Test scores and ability immediately increase after addressing anxiety.
- Over-edgy fear can be used to track and eliminate the causes of anxiety. Fear is your friend.

Case Study

Latt was initially excited to solo, but now he wasn't so sure. He loved playing his oboe but his mouth was so parched that he was worried about being able to play. Did he eat the wrong food for lunch? He drank more water but his mouth was still dry. He was afraid if he drank more he'd have to go to the restroom in the middle of the performance. He didn't know what was wrong or what to do. This made him more nervous than ever.

Case Study

As a make-up artist, Jenny had seen people bond with excitement before the show and she'd seen people blow up at each other. The first actor sat and she started applying his beard and prosthesis. She didn't know what to expect since even people she knew well changed personality a little when they experienced anxiety. She used to be affected but now that she recognized anxiety it was easier to understand the varied reactions she came across. Now others' anxiety didn't affect her much. In fact, she enjoyed using her understanding to quietly calm those she worked with and provide them more than great makeup!

Case Study

LaNara asked her daughter to clean her room, a job that was *long* overdue. LaNara checked in several minutes later. Her daughter had hardly moved. In the past LaNara might have burst out in anger, but now she knew better. She recognized the overwhelmed look. She gently asked, "Do you feel capable of doing this?" Her daughter burst into tears. LaNara gently broke the big job into little tasks. Her daughter progressed quickly and was almost done when a favorite novel surfaced. She stopped cleaning and began to read. LaNara checked and insisted the room be finished first. Soon her daughter was happy and content reading in a completely clean room. It wouldn't be long until her daughter could work independently. [Do you see the difference between anxiety-based procrastination and non-anxiety-based procrastination? When there's anxiety, it's most effective to pull back before pushing forward. When there isn't anxiety, push forward. This process may be necessary when assigning tasks to employees, students, etc. If a task seems too hard, leaders or individuals can break big jobs into smaller tasks. LaNara and her daughter would have saved even more time if this was done immediately.]

Fast Track ReflACTION

1) How have your adrenals helped you in positive ways this week?

_____

_____

_____

2) What physical, mental, emotional and/or behavioral fear symptoms have you seen in yourself; what subtle fear symptoms might be missed that may be impacting you?

_____

_____

_____

3) What could keep you from noticing fear *in the moment*; why is noticing fear in the moment particularly important?

_____

_____

_____

Journal Insights

Write insights regarding the chapter contents. Insights might include how these concepts affect you: feelings about adrenal support, observations regarding edgy and over-edgy fear, possible under-engagement or over engagement due to anxiety, reasons for negative personality changes in self (especially frustration or anger).

_____

_____

_____

_____

_____

_____

_____

_____

Test Yourself
   A. Name five physical symptoms of anxiety.

_____

_____

   B. Name five mental symptoms of anxiety.

_____

_____

   C. Name five emotional symptoms of anxiety.

_____

_____

   D. Name five behavioral symptoms of anxiety.

_____

_____

   E. Some people think they don't have fear but it's as unlikely that a person never has_____ symptoms as it is to _____ have maximum symptoms....It's possible to spot fear in the moment because it _____ different and _____ different.

_____

_____

7. Fix Quick without Quick Fix
Sitting

Empower Yourself
Ignore layers, or…explore layers.

Summary
- Negative feelings initiate protection.
- Negative feelings signal conscious or subconscious safety concerns and increase until heard.
- The intensity of a negative feeling is not always justified.
- Quick fixes are used when emotion is overwhelming.
- Quick fixes are used instead of exploring why an emotion sends an alarm.
- Quick fixes compound problems and combine with triggers. Triggers are past and present emotional reactions combined. They are stronger than the situation merits but have logical origins.
- Triggers and anxiety indicate a conscious or subconscious concern.
- "Hearing the alarm" is solved by sitting with emotion while staying in the present.

- Intergenerational triggers can be overcome.
- Negative emotion loses power when confronted.
- Sitting with emotion (without further arousal, judging, or acting on the emotion) changes the situation from defense to offense.
- There can be good reasons for unsure feelings. Facing fear opens the door to recognizing those reasons.
- There are positives to negative emotion.

Case Study

Cameron patted his horse's flanks and thought, *Okay, this is ridiculous, it's not my first rodeo.* He had been underneath razor-sharp hooves before, why was he suddenly so afraid? Earlier, his sister had teased that perhaps his fear wasn't about the injury at all; maybe it was because he didn't know what he'd do when it was time to retire from the rodeo. He had to admit that the injury brought this concern to the forefront, and the thought of giving up the rodeo scared him almost as much as being trampled by a bull...but was *that* his real concern? Honestly, he couldn't see himself doing anything but rodeo. Emotion surged when he thought about quitting. The surge seemed irrational. Was this something more? His dad passed away a couple of years ago and it still seemed that he watched from the stands. In fact, when Cameron was in the arena he felt closer to his dad than at any other time. It seemed that leaving the rodeo would also mean letting go of this special connection. But then a new thought hit Cameron. His dad had quit the rodeo, too! Cameron let the thought wash over him, and in an instant he felt a new connection with his dad. He swung into the saddle and moved forward. [Cameron faced his fear and discovered layers. Uncovering this type of layered awareness usually takes a few days.]

Case Study

He was late again and dinner was cold again! Mia was not happy as she watched the clock. Collin arrived cheerful, proud of having finished a big project even if it made him a little late. But Mia fumed. He immediately withdrew, "Why are you so upset about this?" When they both cooled down they looked at the situation more rationally. "We've found another intergenerational trigger bump," Mia said. She went on to explain that her grandpa did this to her grandma and it created terrible problems with her grandma's job. Collin admitted that he was programmed to complete projects, even if it meant being late. Collin added, "I'm sorry my trigger bumped into your trigger. I'll try to be more aware." Mia replied, "I'm sorry I made a big deal out of it. Really, I didn't have anything else pressing this evening...Congrats on the project, by the way."

Case Study

Drannon had bad experiences the first three grades of school. His mother hired a tutor because he was now so far behind. The tutor had him work on spelling to increase his reading and writing skills. He became proficient at learning words above his grade level, but still struggled with certain easier words. His tutor explained that this was common in children with backgrounds similar to his and said, "You just have some little 'trigger critters'. Keep scrunching them with 'sure power'. When the trigger critters are all gone your brain will think easy words are easy! Sure power reprograms your brain! It won't replace hard work, but it will help your hard work pay off faster."

Fast Track ReflACTION

1) What negative emotions have you experienced in the last week; what was the warning about?

_____

_____

_____

2) What quick fixes do you commonly use/see? What are the negative side-effects?

_____

_____

_____

3) When could you benefit by sitting with emotion? Do you side-track, what situation or person is blamed?

_____

_____

_____

Journal Insights

Write insights regarding the chapter contents. Insights might include how these concepts affect you: triggers, negative emotion alarms, quick fixes, past experiences affecting reactions, attention to physical and emotional safety.

_____

_____

_____

_____

_____

_____

_____

Test Yourself
    A. What response to emotion unlocks awareness on steroids?

_____

_____

    B. What do you "hit" when you've gone "deep enough" when sitting with emotion and why might it seem weird?

_____

_____

    C. When do most triggers start and why?

_____

_____

    D. Name five names for sitting with fear.

_____

_____

    E. What's the difference between sitting with fear to manage vs. to eliminate fear?

_____

_____

8. Progress
Recording

Empower Yourself
Guess about data, or…gather good data.

Summary
- Most performers use records.
- Records track progress and enhance skill development.
- Anxiety records help, as well.
- Haphazard records yield haphazard data.
- The *CPPro-LP* assists in tracking data.
- No matter how anxiety is tracked, think deeply; record simply.
- It's helpful to track what, when, where, why, and how much anxiety.
- Look beyond the obvious. Data reveals patterns.
- Records don't have to take a lot of time to be beneficial.
- You are the only person who can collect your data. Show up for yourself.
- The brain is hardwired to conserve energy.
- Resistance is a form of anxiety. It dampens ability and enjoyment.

- Usually tasks aren't hard; anxiety is hard.
- Awareness grows so that even fleeting anxiety is spotted, which yields ultimate benefits.

Case Study

Kollin shoved the anxiety record in his duffle. Was his coach serious about keeping an anxiety record? Good thing it was only 5 minutes, a couple of times a week, for 6 weeks. And why did his coach insist that records include both practice and games! Who cares about practice? It's the game that counts! Kollin dutifully wrote in the record. *Boring*. But, after three weeks he noticed a pattern. He did well until he made a major mistake. It was downhill after that. This happened in practice and games. Also, he belittled himself a lot. But when he objectively rated his performance, he did well in both practice and games. Wow, he had no idea how much he focused on his mistakes! Knowing this made it easier to work on self-improvement without self-criticism. He became more consistent. Crashes became rare. How weird was that? Okay, maybe his coach wasn't completely crazy about keeping the record!

Case Study

Chrysta's busy schedule was so tight that she thought an anxiety record was impossible. But as she sat in the parking lot waiting for a friend she decided to use her phone's voice recorder to write down some observations. One insight led to another. In the five minutes she recognized several symptoms she hadn't realized before. But even better, she felt stronger. She had no idea what a difference it would make to actually write down her thoughts, even if dictated to the phone. It was like a string of sausages. Once she tugged an insight and got it written, others followed. She decided it was worth making time for more formal observations. She slipped a pad into her bag and jotted thoughts periodically. She had to admit that she hadn't really paid much attention to her feelings besides just coping. Now she was more thoughtful and observant.

Case Study

Okay, first of all Suzanne was surprised to realize she had anxiety! She might have been upset to learn this, but the record also showed that her anxiety wasn't very bad. Now that she understood more about anxiety and knew herself better she could be proactive about addressing it so that it didn't cause problems or grow.

Fast Track ReflACTION
1) When do you experience resistance anxiety? How can you reduce the drag? (Resistance is common when getting up in the morning, resuming a task after a break, etc.)

_____

_____

2) How does anxiety awareness give you an edge; why is awareness in the moment an even bigger edge?

_____

_____

_____

3) What anxiety factors and patterns do you suspect/observe; how can recognizing patterns reduce anxiety?

_____

_____

_____

Journal Insights

Write insights regarding the chapter contents. Insights might include how these concepts affect you: notice what, when, where, why and how much in relation to the physical, mental, emotional and behavioral fear symptoms. What records are already used like attendance, grades, timed data, etc. do they affect anxiety.

_____

_____

_____

_____

_____

_____

_____

Test Yourself

A. The benefits of a record are experienced after how many weeks and how much total time; what's done after that?

_____

_____

B. There are _____ (fill in) reasons for anxiety, performance improvement, or decline. How can progress be faster after a slump?

_____

_____

C. Observations are noted during what two times and why?

_____

_____

D. What seems to slide over the brain when "insignificant" anxiety limits ability?

_____

_____

E. What kind of data is not very helpful, and why?

_____

_____

9. Treasure Hunt
Searching

Empower Yourself
Reactively respond, or…proactively prevent.

Summary
- A proactive stance can minimize performance problems and help avoid performance disasters.
- Outcome anxiety is very specific to certain situations, people, conditions or skills.
- Anxiety is common in high-stakes situations, females, and the most and least capable.
- The most capable hide anxiety better but crash worse when overwhelmed.
- Reoccurring problems allow patterns to be identified. Insights usually come in layers.
- Identifying patterns helps in eliminating problems. Records maximize awareness.
- Awareness allows a person to react proactively.

Case Study

Naddie was a news reporter. She had absolutely no performance anxiety in front of the camera and didn't think a record would be beneficial. But she kept one on a whim. To her surprise she found a pattern. She was uncomfortable reading names. At times the insecurities about names affected other parts of her job. This reduced when she became aware. She then proactively adjusted her preparation to include attention to names and phonetic spelling. She wasn't going to take a chance on disaster! She felt much more secure. Her record helped to identify and reverse the one thing that held her back. [The record helped improve performance and preparation. Her core was strengthened.]

Case Study

Ken was having a great game. But then he spotted last year's top player who graduated and had come back to visit. Suddenly Ken's ability declined. Later, as he kept his record he realized this happened whenever a better player walked in. Oh wait! There was a pattern. It meant a lot to him to impress someone who was better. He could well play in front of anyone else. In fact, it seemed ironic that it was the good players who caused anxiety for him, not the influential non-athlete dignitaries or wealthy sponsors. This was good info to know. If he could play well in some situations, certainly he could do well in all situations.

Case Study

Dee performed all the time and didn't have any trouble singing or public speaking. In fact, it was kind of fun. He played piano, too. But *that* was a different story! He could accompany okay if it was group singing. But he'd long since given up on trying to get ALL the notes right. He just didn't seem to have that skill and chalked it up to lack of practice (even though it was still a problem despite times he'd practiced well.) He never considered that he had bad performance anxiety because most performing was so easy. He didn't know that anxiety was specific to the task. Once he realized this he found improvement easier, although his keyboard skills initially lagged behind his other performance skills.

Fast Track ReflACTION

1) Do you experience apprehensions during some activities or school subjects and not others? Which? Why?

_____

_____

_____

2) Do you experience apprehensions in parts of an activity and not other parts; which parts, why? (For example, a baseball player might feel more comfortable catching a fly verses a ground ball; it might be because of a lack of practice, a bad experience, or an injury.)

_____

_____

_____

3) Scan the chapter and list the categories you fit in (younger vs. older; female vs. male, gifted vs. struggling, anxiety in all activities vs. isolated parts of some activities, etc.) What factors or patterns emerge?

_____

_____

_____

Journal Insights

Write insights regarding the chapter contents. Insights might include how these concepts affect you: most and least gifted, parent with anxiety, insecurity spreads, factors or patterns affecting ability, when do you feel uncomfortable.

_____

_____

_____

_____

_____

_____

_____

Test Yourself

    A. Anxiety can grow _____ a person or _____ people; how can this be stopped?

_____

_____

    B. How is anxiety in the least and most gifted the same and different?

_____

_____

    C. What is the key to getting maximum benefit from noting and recording observations?

_____

_____

    D. Awareness is not just performance enhancing, what else does it change?

_____

_____

    E. What *specific* types of situations can be high-stakes? Name three.

_____

_____

10. Got Your Brain
Functioning

Empower Yourself
Disregard brain function, or…recognize brain function.

Summary
- Trying to perform without the brain is hard.
- Anxiety management usually focuses on the *content* of thoughts. Functional brain support focuses on thought *construction*.
- Functional thought construction immediately increases learning rates during practice and quality output during performance.
- Attention to thought sensations produces immediate benefits that increase over time.
- Brain micro-shutdowns are responsible for a lot of performance anxiety and flow/zone problems.
- Adrenaline in the blood not only goes to the body, it goes to the brain. High emotion slows and even stops the learning centers of the brain.
- Performance and practice pressure can elevate emotion and affect brain function.

- Brain shorting is a lack of continuous brain function, resulting in a lack of continuous thought. This is not a loss of *focus*; it's a loss of *function*.
- There are three types of brain shorting: crunching—fight, fogging—flight, blanking—freeze. They correlate to mentally pushing through, pulling back, and the inability to process.
- Micro blanks can be almost undetectable, especially if other highly-refined skills compensate.
- Even capable individuals experience improved outcomes when thinking improves.

Case Study

All these years, Jadley thought her brain processed music notes so quickly that she simply skimmed them. What a shock to learn that she wasn't reading the notes at all—she was playing by ear! Honestly, it was a relief to finally understand why she had difficulty sight reading and what to do about it. She changed her practice strategy. Instead of focusing on the notes, she focused on brain sensations and continually considered, "How does my brain feel? Is it processing?" She learned to sense how her brain felt when actually reading versus playing by ear. She was surprised that sometimes she crunched and sometimes she fogged. She expected that her sight reading would improve, but did not expect that *everything* would improve. Wow! Who would have thought that focusing on brain sensations instead of notes would cause such a breakthrough! (Jadley told two college friends, who then had similar success applying brain awareness to volleyball and test taking.)

Case Study

Oh no! Here came the hard part. Ada locked her concentration and braced herself. She was determined to get through this. She held her breath. Her muscles got tense. Whew, made it! She hated that section. She would either mess up or barely skim through.

Case Study

Cindy disliked distributing things to co-workers when her boss was watching. It was nerve racking. It was like all their names went out the window and as she became even more nervous she looked like an incompetent idiot. It was embarrassing and she felt like her boss looked down on her. She wanted him to understand that she wasn't always like this! It just happened when she was under pressure.

Fast Track ReflACTION

1) When have you experienced (or observed) crunching, fogging, or blanking?

2) In what subjects or activities do you "struggle," and how could better brain function benefit you?

_____

_____

_____

3) In what subjects or activities do you "strut," and how could better brain function benefit you?

_____

_____

_____

Journal Insights

Write insights regarding the chapter contents. Insights might include how these concepts affect you: tension in the mind or body, how thoughts feel, parts of brain felt, times when thoughts flow and when they don't.

_____

_____

_____

_____

_____

_____

_____

_____

Test Yourself

    A. What can occur in very capable individuals who have no fear sensation, recovery quickly, and compensate well; why?

_____

_____

    B. Why does thinking about thought formation sensations work better to fix focus than thinking about focus?

_____

_____

    C. Performance (and practice) pressure can have what effect on the brain?

_____

_____

    D. Many people try to perform without what; what fluctuates?

_____

_____

    E. Most brain support concentrates on the _____ of a thought; but functional brain support concentrates on the _____ of a thought?

_____

_____

11. Bring Your Brain
Increasing

Empower Yourself
Neglect your brain, or…train your brain.

Summary
- Better performance starts with better brain support during practice.
- It's impossible to eliminate performance anxiety if brain shorting disrupts flow. Crunching, fogging, and blanking can be fixed
- *Crunching:* The brain is overactive. Release mental tension. Mental tension is counterproductive. Practice until a task can be done comfortably without a change in mental sensation.
- *Fogging:* The brain is underactive. Stimulate the brain. Counter uncertainty. Fogging tends to expand and cause uncertainty in mastered things. Students who flounder almost always have brain fogging. Grades and ability shoot up when it is addressed. It's easier to do things with the brain.
- *Blanking:* The brain is not processing. Develop the habit of being calm. Tension shuts down the brain. Mistakes usually happen during brain shorting. Watch for compensating skills.

- Build brain support. Start low pressure and low difficulty, and then increase to high pressure and high difficulty *while maintaining mental flow*. Eliminating brain shorting feels slow at first, but it's fast overall.
- Notice unsure feelings. Addressing unsure feelings is not touchy-feely, boggy-down stuff. It's awareness and new focus.
- No matter how smart or talented you are, you can't perform without your brain.

Case Study

Kenna had performed all her life. She was very successful, and never had stage fright. When she learned about brain shorting she was curious and decided to check brain sensations and breathing. To her amazement, she realized she did have performance anxiety, but *only* during practice and *only* when memorizing new material! Her brain was taking "micro coffee breaks" that slowed memorization. She said, "A great performance starts with confidence in practice. My confidence went up when I discovered I had performance anxiety! How ironic is that! I thought I didn't have a good memory, but actually, I didn't have good mental flow. Everything has been better since I learned I had performance anxiety and worked on it. Who'd have thought!" (And then she giggled realizing that the problem *was* thought!)

Case Study

Royce laughed, "Yah I get it, I just don't want to do it right now." As soon as everyone looked away he glanced back at the math problem. He had no idea what to do. He understood it earlier but when it came time to do the assignment it was like everything was gone. Then a friend cornered him in private, "Hey, every time I ask, you say things are fine but you're the last one done. Level with me." Royce admitted he struggled. Royce's friend didn't leave when he joked. In fact, if he joked his friend stayed focused and pointed things out. Royce's confidence and focus increased.

Case Study

Lulee was constantly applauded for her skills. But walking in her office you'd think she was inept! When asked about the piles she said she didn't have time for sorting papers. But when she learned about brain fogging she recognized it in herself. She hated making decisions and paperwork was replete with them. She decided to use her office as a "brain-training boot camp". Each day she spent only fifteen minutes (so as not to become overwhelmed) and sorted a small stack of papers. She was especially mindful of brain sensations and countered any frustration or nebulous feelings. Within a few weeks her office was pristine, but more importantly, the clarity carried over into how she approached life. As she addressed the things she had avoided her life became more balanced and enjoyable.

Fast Track ReflACTION

1) Do you experience crunching, fogging, or blanking? Consider both performance and non-performance situations. What is a helpful intervention? (Try it.)

_____

_____

_____

2) Name a skill you would like to improve, outline a low skill/low pressure to high skill/high pressure plan to increase flow. (Try it.)

_____

_____

_____

3) What short-term and long-term problems have you experienced that may be eliminated by paying attention to brain shorting *sensations* and thought *flow*?

_____

_____

_____

Journal Insights

Write insights regarding the chapter contents. Insights might include how these concepts affect you: where do mistakes usually happen, how to use low pressure/ low stakes to high pressure/high stakes, what does brain fight/flight/freeze feel like.

_____

_____

_____

_____

_____

_____

_____

_____

Test Yourself

    A. Increased mental tension does not equate with what?

_____

_____

    B. Released tension does not mean to diminish what two things; in fact, what increases with comfortable flow?

_____

_____

    C. What teaches the brain to stop functioning and should not be used to mask brain fogging?

_____

_____

    D. Spotting brain sensations works because it's working on more than brain flow. What else is it?

_____

_____

    E. What do you watch for when learning to spot micro-blanking?

_____

_____

12. Plan a Neuroplasticity Party
Building

Empower Yourself
Accept what you have, or…build what you need.

Summary
- The brain can be shaped.
- Neural pathways can be developed or pruned.
- It takes about three weeks of consistent effort.
- The fact that it takes effort to change is a protection that makes change possible.
- Some tasks require new brain structures and need extra persistence.
- Neural pathways do not discern good or bad quality. They reinforce what they're given.
- Negative things develop negative connections, so use care to reinforce positive connections.
- Deliberately shrinking problems and good habits can propel a person forward.
- Mental practice/visualization improves ability.

- Kinesthetic visualization is the most powerful type of visualization.
- First person and third person visualization have different uses and benefits.
- Anything can improve through neuroplasticity—plan a party and watch the improvement.

Case Study

This case study happened to me. I was the director of a play when an actress dropped out 2 ½ weeks before the show. No replacement could be found so I jumped in. I wasn't worried because I was a seasoned performer before becoming a director and choreographer. But as I attempted to memorize, nothing stuck and I definitely became unsure of coming out okay. I persisted. In the end, the first half-page took over two weeks and the last half-page took only a few minutes. At the time, I thought that I had finally put in enough time. But later I realized that the timeline coincided with neuroplasticity research, and that neural pathways were probably involved to some extent. (I also realized that directing and acting are as different as conducting an orchestra and playing an instrument. This would also be true of an athlete switching team positions or a business person being promoted, etc. Even when activities are related, the mental skills may be different, hence the need for neuroplasticity.)

Case Study

A world-class organist related that while working on a PhD in Europe his teacher mentioned the benefits of mental practice away from the organ. So that week the student split time equally between practicing at the organ and practicing in his mind. The next lesson his teacher was astounded by the progress and asked what had been done differently. When the organist became a professor himself, he advocated the benefits of careful, engaged mental practice to increase the speed of improvement.

Case Study

Lily Ann had been away on an extended vacation for over a month. Whew, she was tired at the end of the first day back! Why was it so hard? She thought it was due to getting back into the swing of things. But she deliberately planned her vacation in the slow season and she had relatively little to do compared to the busy season. It didn't make sense, oh wait. Was this the effect of neuroplasticity? She'd read about it on the plane in an article. Her thoughts were rudely interrupted by a spider crawling across her desk. She was afraid of spiders. Instead of bounding away and calling someone she decided to try the new skills she'd learned in the same article. She immediately used the new techniques that disrupted old patterns. The critter was still there exploring a paper but as long as she kept the sensation of being in charge she managed to take the paper outside and let the spider go. [Some immediately experience changes in fear responses, others develop the ability to disrupt old patterns and confront fears step by step.]

Fast Track ReflACTION

1) If you had a neuroplasticity party, what would you like to change and how would you do it? (Try it.)

_____

_____

_____

2) Imagine doing a task "first person" and again "third person;" how could you use each to improve your ability? (Try it.)

_____

_____

_____

3) When might mental practice be more beneficial for you than physical practice? (Try it.)

_____

_____

_____

Journal Insights

Write insights regarding the chapter contents. Insights might include how these concepts affect you: thoughts being reinforced, beneficial mental improvements, use of neuroplasticity, brain function during performance.

_____

_____

_____

_____

_____

_____

_____

Test Yourself

    A. About how long does it take to establish a new neural pathway and why is this a protection?

_____

_____

    B. Why doesn't positive change happen more often? Name four reasons.

_____

_____

    C. To improve most quickly focus on the _____ of a task?

_____

_____

    D. What are some common names for warming up neural pathways from the examples of the basketball player, actor, speaker, skier, musician?

_____

_____

    E. What was mentioned that is done mentally to _decrease_ something?

_____

_____

13. When Not To Think
Trusting

Empower Yourself
Think and sink, or…release the think.

Summary

- Conscious improvement comes from the left frontal lobe in the brain; this is helpful in practice.
- Automated responses and memory (including muscle memory) come from the right hemisphere in the brain; this is helpful in performance.
- Learned skills shift from the left frontal lobe to the right hemisphere. Memory-based performance relies heavily on right hemisphere automation. Shifting back to the left frontal lobe in performance can be detrimental.
- "Choking" is often caused by a brain shift, this lessens with experience. The left frontal lobe discerns quality, and the right hemisphere accepts what's put in. Imperfect practice puts an imperfect performance into the right hemisphere. This is either spit out as is, or the frontal lobe attempts to correct during performance. Either way, there's trouble.

- Practicing poorly is "I'll-fix-it-later procrastination." Performing as you have practiced encourages quality practice and develops the ability to use desired brain functions on command. Only perfect practice makes perfect, so practice quality. A beginner can look like a professional doing easy skills.
- Quality practice increases learning ability and confidence. There are quirky things that can engage the right hemisphere and improve performance. Brains need breaks.
- Quality performance involves optimal use of the left frontal lobe and the right hemisphere during practice and performance.

Case Study

Brach was a defensive lineman and loved reading the offense. He was very diligent about developing skills during practice; but then, in games he felt torn between technique and his gut instinct. One day he missed a couple of tackles, and in frustration he just went with his gut. Suddenly he was nailing everything. He laughed inside—he'd never considered that thinking less could improve his game. He prepared carefully. But in games he seemed to do better if he trusted his gut.

Case Study

Last quarter wasn't as good. Arial had waited to study for the finals until they were upon her. This quarter was different. She studied all along and treated each chapter quiz like a final. When finals came not only was studying easier, she seemed to remember the material better after the finals were over.

Case Study

Nerves were building. It was understandable, this audition was important. Charie said to herself, "Okay, just sing like you're in the shower! Time for autopilot. No changes. No improvements." She stepped up and went straight for the familiar sensations from practice.

Fast Track ReflACTION
1) What mental or muscle memory does your type of performances require?

_____

_____

_____

2) What practice changes would send a better performance package to your right hemisphere?

_____

_____

_____

3) What can you do to maximize performing what you practiced rather than changing during performance?

_____

_____

_____

Journal Insights

Write insights regarding the chapter contents. Insights might include how these concepts affect you: when is your right hemisphere and left frontal lobe used, when do you improve, what causes frustration, what breaks are needed.

_____

_____

_____

_____

_____

_____

_____

_____

Test Yourself

    A. Why are brain shifts from the left frontal lobe to the right hemisphere good?

    B. Why can conscious awareness be detrimental in performance when skills are re-analyzed and mastered material shifts back?

    C. "Choking" isn't usually a personality or preparation problem; it's what?

    D. What kind of practice makes perfect?

    E. Name two reasons why "I'll-fix-it-later-procrastination" is detrimental in *practice*.

---

14. Glucose and Grudge Busting
Supporting

Empower Yourself
Mindless default, or…mindful choice.

Summary
- Trillions of brain cells and connections communicate through neurotransmitters. Neurotransmitters are made from glucose.
- The brain uses about 20% of consumed glucose. Glucose doesn't always burn at the same rate. Unpleasant activities burn more glucose, pleasant ones burn less.
- Refined glucose causes blood sugar spikes and lows. Powering through is counterproductive. Self nourishment enables more effective engagement. Glucose equals willpower. Doing things grudgingly burns glucose faster.
- When every other freedom is denied, there is still a choice about attitude. Engaging while mindfully and cheerfully aware of choice is different than pushing through mindlessly unaware.
- The brain is preprogrammed to protect and instinctively pull back.

- 'Grudge busting" is a safety valve. This choice involves evaluation of what can and can't be done.
- There are two learning pathways in the brain. Negative emotions engage the traumatic/low-road pathway while positive emotions engage the transformational/high-road pathway. Transformational learning results in quality learning.
- A choice to be cheerful and mindful is a choice to use the brain effectively.

Case Study

Catherin was tired of being ineffective. She made a spreadsheet of everything she wanted to accomplish in the month. Each morning she noticed her "protective brain" pulling her away from her new goals and healthy habits. She said to herself, "I can only omit things if I really don't want the benefits. And if I want the benefits I have to start *immediately* and complete each item quickly and cheerfully!" Her energy improved and productivity soared. She confessed that sometimes she did omit things or rearrange her schedule. But she felt that the reason she was so effective was that she switched from "unplanned, irritable, default mode" to "pre-planned, upbeat, choices mode".

Case Study

"Sweetheart, I know you think you can miss lunch, grab a caffeine boost, and everything is just fine, but have you noticed how differently you interact when you arrive home? You're grumpy! Maybe *you* can manage missing a meal, but I'm not sure *we* can. If it's all the same, I'd like to pack a few healthy foods you can eat at your desk. I figure it's an easy way to get my great guy back."

Case Study

Ruth had a lot to memorize in a short time and doubted she could. Initially she didn't recognize her doubt. But a friend said she was good at memorizing. Ruth decided to focus on that thought, "I'll be okay. I'm good at memorizing." Wow, retention was *immediately* easier! Shortly afterward she learned about low-level and high-level thinking. Suddenly it all made sense! She told her friend that when she doubted herself the memorized material actually felt like a tense lump in her brain. But her brain seemed to relax and the material "spread out" when she believed in herself and stopped berating herself for waiting to start. There were definite brain sensations she hadn't noticed before.

Fast Track ReflACTION

1) How have glucose levels and hydration affected you today?

_____

_____

2) How could you more mindfully and cheerfully engage; what would be the benefits? Are there things you should respectfully disengage from; what would be the benefits?

_____

_____

_____

3) When do you experience low-level thinking; how can you maximize high-level thinking, and what would be the benefits?

_____

_____

_____

Journal Insights

Write insights regarding the chapter contents. Insights might include how these concepts affect you: how physical things affect emotional things, how attitude affects your body, what is more productive than grudges, when you experience high-level and low-level learning.

_____

_____

_____

_____

_____

_____

_____

Test Yourself

    A. A choice to maintain _____, _____, and _____ is really a choice to live life more _____ and _____.

_____

_____

    B. Why does glucose = willpower?

_____

_____

    C. Name three ways that caring for physical health is actually caring for emotional health.

_____

_____

    D. Viktor Frankl said that when all other freedoms are denied one thing remains, what is that freedom and how does it affect energy for performance?

_____

_____

    E. The brain comes pre-programmed to pull back, this makes it easy for what to take over?

_____

_____

15. Heart Attacking
Realizing

Empower Yourself
Repress your heart, or…restore your heart.

Summary
- Thinking involves the brain and body. The heart and brain are more connected than realized, the heart can override the brain.
- Flow/zone is affected by emotional memories that appear embedded in tissue that either directly or indirectly affect the heart.
- A heart-brain link was discovered by specialists and athletes increasing flow/zone; education and yoga show similar trauma connections.
- When memories and anxieties are processed, there are documented positive changes to the heart and lungs. Even more minor things that would not be considered traumatic can affect ability.
- The heart can stimulate the amygdala. The heart-brain connection can be trained. The connection is likely affected right now as you learn.
- Processing is recognizing and understanding thoughts and feelings and may help lift the negative impact of memories out of cells in a way that improves overall ability.

- Sometimes great effort is made to improve ability without attention to emotional things and their impact on the body. High-level athletes have trained the heart-brain connection to improve ability.

Case Study

Dart's cycling race speeds had dropped. He was inexplicably slowing down in the turns. He had heard that biofeedback coupled with counseling could help. In counseling, a couple of minor incidents were discovered that affected his race. When he was a boy, he was riding down the street when his mother suddenly screamed. From her vantage, she thought a car was going to hit him. Though he was safe, this brief moment was recorded in his memory. Later, he saw someone skid out while turning in a race. He'd seen racers skid out before, it was common. But for some reason these experiences mentally linked and his turns slowed. Though these two memories were relatively insignificant, they negatively impacted his output. Once they were identified and processed, Dart's race speeds shot up—not just on the turns, but through the entire race

Case Study

Caryn, a woodwind player, was having difficulty with air in the short phrases, let alone the long ones. She had recently experienced extreme trauma. A therapist recommended yoga for emotional centering and exercise. Each day at the end of the DVD "chakra clearing" session, there was a meditation chant which she did not have enough air to complete in one breath. She was discouraged thinking it would take significant cardio training to get her air control back. The introduction to the DVD heart chakra session said that heart and lung capacity could increase when "cleared." She doubted it. At the end of the exercise session, she did the chant as usual. But she was astounded to complete it in one breath! She replayed the chant and then kept going to see how long she could go. She almost did two full chants in one breath! She could hardly wait for her next music rehearsal! [She was told that if a chakra isn't blocked, differences are not noted; it's believed that issues can affect function in any chakra, but trauma is said to especially affect the heart chakra.]

Case Study

Nita was calm and collected. Cal was boisterous and energetic. The marriage worked but there were definite emotional differences! They thought it was simply a difference in personality, but after learning about brain structure they wondered if it were something else, or perhaps brain structure helped determine personality! In any event, Nita said she enjoyed deeper emotion when sensing it through Cal's exuberance; and Cal said he sensed the ability to react calmly when considering Nita's reactions.

Fast Track ReflACTION
1) When have you sensed emotions overriding your brain; what might be causing this?

_____

_____

_____

2) What type of brain and heart function did you apparently inherit; how does it influence your emotional responses?

_____

_____

_____

3) Processing involves noticing fleeing insights or ideas. What fleeting thoughts have you had this week that may be beneficial to further consider?

_____

_____

_____

Journal Insights

Write insights regarding the chapter contents. Insights might include how these concepts affect you: what past experiences affect your heart, the possible brain structure you were born with, what positive and negative body changes affect ability, benefits of balance and core stamina.

_____

_____

_____

_____

_____

_____

_____

Test Yourself

   A. What are the two types of "cardioplasticity"?

_____

_____

   B. Yoga masters and researchers identify an interplay between, _____, _____, and _____ that affect the capacity of the _____ and _____.

_____

_____

   C. Those with anxiety tend to have high emotional input from _____ and _____, and less _____ override.

_____

_____

   D. Traditionally it was thought that the brain controlled the heart. Name three of several unexpected things about the heart?

_____

_____

   E. Most believe that thinking is done by the brain but the book says that thinking comes from what_____.

_____

_____

16. A Change of Heart
Improving

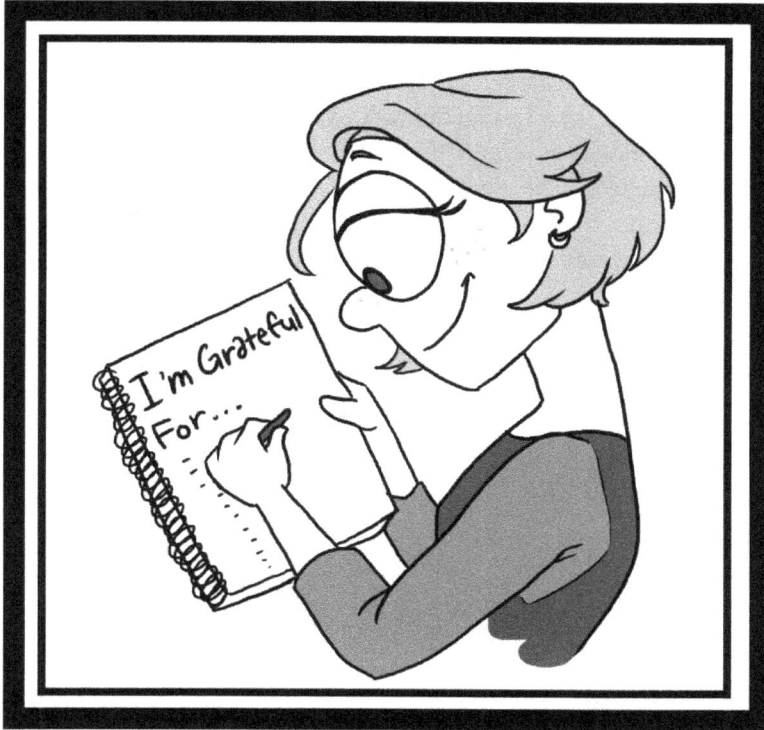

Empower Yourself
Deadbeat, or…elite heartbeat.

Summary
- There are physical and emotional baselines that affect how the body and mind react. The body maintains baselines through physical and emotional homeostasis. Anything out of a normal baseline puts the body and brain on alert, even positive changes.
- Triggers cause stronger reactions (like anxiety) and indicate an "emotional ouch" that needs attention. Triggers can affect physical energy even when a person is calm. Addressing negative triggers permanently improves the heartbeat pattern.
- The heart can't generally be controlled, but breath can be controlled, and it affects the heart. Deep gratitude, genuine service, yoga, and visualized energy states also improve ability and heart function.
- The electromagnetic field caused by one heart is known to affect the heartbeats of others nearby.
- A study showed that choir heartbeats synchronized when singing.

- Heart research introduces a new dimension to team work, the influence of an audience, and the concept of being of "one heart." While further research will clarify the scope of these theories, current research supports the benefits of changing one's heart.

Case Study

Valerie felt her emotion rising, but she wasn't too worried. Though it was the championship match, she had been working on skills that she knew would reduce her nervousness. She sat in a quiet place, deeply breathed and thought of one thing after another that she was truly thankful for. She had made it this far! She was healthy! It was a beautiful day! Her grandpa traveled to see her! She liked this court! She had eyes and could see! She had hands and could use them! She made a game of finding more and more things to be grateful for, and then feeling the gratitude more and more deeply. As she did, she realized how many things she took for granted and how insignificant this championship was in comparison with the rest of life. When she stepped on the court, she felt grounded and empowered. She was completely ready to enjoy the moment!

Case Study

Brenda first visited her widowed neighbor as a courtesy. The periodic visits stretched into months and now Brenda visited for an entirely different reason. They had become friends. What initially seemed like a duty was now a pleasure. The gratitude was two-way. Her neighbor appreciated the things Brenda helped with and Brenda appreciated her neighbor's wise perspective and friendship. Brenda didn't expect to have a close friend forty years older! She also didn't expect that the service would become so enjoyable.

Case Study

Bryce opened the door and exuberantly exclaimed, "Wow, we had a great crowd at the show tonight! It was a lot of fun!" His roommate glanced up from his book, "I'm glad. Our volleyball crowd was a serious drag. Not many, all quiet! Wish they were like last week's rowdies; they were great."

Fast Track ReflACTION

1) What emotional and physical baselines would you like to change; how could you do it?

_____

_____

_____

2) Take several sincere gratitude breaths and reflect on the benefits; what might routine gratitude breaths or other heart-changing activities yield? (Try it.)

_____

_____

_____

3) In a typical week, when would you most benefit from deliberately changing emotional energy states to be more of "one heart" with someone; what might be the benefits? (Try it.)

_____

_____

_____

Journal Insights

Write insights regarding the chapter contents. Insights might include how these concepts affect you: levels of gratitude, possible yoga, opportunities for service, awareness of energy, how the heart feels emotionally.

_____

_____

_____

_____

_____

_____

_____

Test Yourself

    A. What happened when the Swedish choir sang while their hearts were monitored and what did the director hypothesize?

_____

_____

    B. What is said to "clear" chakras in 20-30 minutes and appears to yield short- and long-term physiological benefits?

_____

_____

    C. What is necessary for service to be beneficial; what causes it to be detrimental?

_____

_____

    D. What can be said and done if an extremely difficult, traumatic, or criminal situation makes gratitude difficult?

_____

_____

    E. Expressing sincere gratitude even if a situation is crappy attunes a person to _____ and balances _____ out?

_____

_____

17. Culture Shock
Comprehending

Empower Yourself
Deny saturation, or…devour inspiration.

Summary
- Technology's impact on culture has resulted in huge advantages and disadvantages. Higher stress is the new normal.
- Technology's impact has changed cultural expectations. Performers are now compared to world standards; previously they were only compared to local standards.
- Comparisons are made to things that are not even possible in real time due to extensive editing and enhancing. Personal comparisons are frequently made to fictional things.
- The negative result of technology is pressure. The positive result is inspiration. Inspiration strengthens the core.
- Information overload weakens the core. Technology addiction affects the brain like drug addiction.
- Technology also provides resources that save time and energy, so there is time to pursue inspiration.

- There are unlimited benefits from technology and one primary detriment: pressure. Pressure is a choice.
- Attention to thoughts and feelings results in the ability to make good choices and maximize the benefits of technology.

Case Study

Laura wanted some fresh dance lifts to put in her choreography. She searched online and within seconds was thumbing through YouTube videos. She posted links so her dancers could analyze and envision before rehearsal. Even though rehearsal was in just a few hours, she knew they'd all see the group post on their phones. Rehearsal was going to be fun; these were great lifts! Now to *immediately* get off YouTube and Facebook before getting sucked in! Otherwise she wouldn't get her choreography or paperwork done.

Case Study

The pressure was on! It was the last crack at this opportunity—they only allowed three tries at this exam. Mary used to crumble when the pressure was this high. But she decided that her life had many possible paths and that if one thing didn't work out something wonderful would, even if it was a different path. When she gratefully put things in perspective instead of feeling overwhelmed and burdened, she felt energized. "Bring it on! Let's see how things turn out!"

Case Study

Diane loved to create and nothing was more fun than browsing the internet! Sometimes she closed feeling rejuvenated but other times she felt depressed. She began to pay more attention to thoughts and feelings. She was rejuvenated when she hadn't spent too much time online and when she got fresh ideas to enhance her creativity. She was depressed when she got sucked in and neglected other responsibilities especially if she compared herself to what she saw. Oh! That was easy to fix! She took more responsibility to monitor herself. Simple choices maximized her pleasure.

Fast Track ReflACTION
1) Name something, only available this generation, that positively impacted you this week and how you can maximize the benefits.

_____

_____

_____

2) Name something, only available this generation, that negatively impacted you this week and how you can minimize the detriments.

_____

_____

_____

3) How does awareness of the impact of your choices give you an edge in a technological culture?

_____

_____

_____

Journal Insights

Write insights regarding the chapter contents. Insights might include how these concepts affect you: does technology increase or decrease your pressure, are there problems from conscious or subconscious comparisons, what inspiration would be helpful to seek, how would your current talents and abilities be viewed in a small community 150 years ago.

_____

_____

_____

_____

_____

_____

_____

Test Yourself

   A. Of the earth's history, how many generations have had access to recorded performances; before that, what were the only kind of performances?

_____

_____

   B. Name three types of possible comparisons to fictional things from the book.

_____

_____

   C. Name three positive and three negative things mentioned in the book that are a result of technology.

_____

_____

   D. According to this chapter, is stress always bad, why or why not?

_____

_____

   E. Give three names for too much information, how does this potentially impact performance?

_____

_____

18. Stop Trying to Get it Right
Rising

Empower Yourself
Obediently conform, or…intelligently explore.

Summary
- Those with outcome anxiety often try to do things "right."
- The "right" mentality increases pressure, stifles learning, hints at perfectionism, and crushes creativity.
- Ultimately, there is no "right" way. Even top experts can disagree. And opinions change as improvements are made.
- Careful training and practice is a means to an end, not the end-all. Traditional ways of doing things are tools to build on.
- Interpretation, technique, style, artistry, timing, rules, and strategy are subjective and change.
- Rules are learned in order to break them intelligently (except competition rules).
- Training is not to teach conformity but creativity.
- Those who chase doing things "right" may stifle their own contributions.
- Someday your way may be the "right way."

Case Study

Anne moved across the country to train and was surprised to find that what they considered to be "right" was completely different from what she had learned. There were even different names for moves. In time she found that exposure to both types of training enhanced her ability. It gave her an edge. She had more tools to work with.

Case Study

Ryan hadn't had private coaching for a while. When he returned, everything had changed. The new way was better, but a decade of muscle memory was already trained into his muscles. It was frustrating, but he got to work. After a few months, he was proficient in the new technique. He confessed that retraining was tough, but worth it.

Case Study

In a national teachers' workshop, one professional concert pianist encouraged scales that crawled sideways up the piano using two fingers. Another professor introduced an innovative "flattened" technique to reduce injuries common to pianists. Another suggested that non-career students abandon technique altogether and just enjoy making music. Teachers determined what was "right" for their students.

Fast Track ReflACTION

1) In what ways would you benefit from trying harder to do things "right"?

_____

_____

_____

2) In what ways would you benefit from not being as concerned about doing things "right"?

_____

_____

_____

3) What specific change could improve technique, inspire creativity, and release pressure for you?

_____

_____

_____

Journal Insights

Write insights regarding the chapter contents. Insights might include how these concepts affect you: how and why you conform or don't conform, if efforts to please hamper discoveries, how carefully you train, times to break rules intelligently.

_____

_____

_____

_____

_____

_____

_____

_____

Test Yourself

   A. What cranks up stress (it's addressed throughout this chapter)?

_____

_____

   B. What rules should not be broken; what rules could be broken?

_____

_____

   C. Name five people or companies in this chapter who rose to the top of their field by not doing things "right".

_____

_____

   D. Name three factors that can overcome the "wrong" timing.

_____

_____

   E. Traditional correctness shouldn't be abandoned, but too much emphasis on *complying* can do what three things?

_____

_____

19. Appearance Anxiety
Releasing

Empower Yourself
Appearance depletion, or…reasonable completion.

Summary

- Appearance anxiety about hair, clothes, car, house, education, job or status is outcome anxiety—unsure of coming out okay.
- Obsession about appearance usually affects other areas of performance.
- Appearance anxiety clouds judgment.
- The "right" appearance varies.
- All appearance anxiety is tied to perfectionism—perfectly imperfect (grungy), perfectly perfect (pristine), perfectly worried in between.
- Discomfort regarding the "perfect" look drives behavior.
- Appearance anxiety may manifest in avoiding people or situations, meticulous social media editing, and passing up opportunities.
- Appearance doesn't solve self-worth anxieties; meeting primary needs does. Businesses exploit appearance anxiety and pseudo primary needs.
- Time, energy, and money are drained. Greatness doesn't have to be right.

- An understanding of appearance anxiety allows a person to be authentic, adapt, and make decisions truly in their favor. Appearance anxiety is eliminated by becoming aware, authentically meeting primary needs, and making reasonable choices.
- Anticipating what others think (even if their reaction is positive) gives away core power. Genuine confidence comes from being okay with reasonable decisions.

Case Study

Karalyn was in the boutique on a mission. She was determined to get a great outfit for the regional meeting. It was the first big meeting since she was promoted, and she wanted to make a good impression. She pulled a couple of suits off the rack and proceeded to the dressing room. But as she looked more carefully, they were similar to other things she owned. Why spend the time and energy to try them on? What she really needed was a crisp blouse and a new purse since hers was getting worn. On her way to the cash register she spotted some great accessories. They'd be out of style soon, so she chose only one. She didn't labor over the decision since she wanted to get home and enjoy a hot bath with a great book. The next day she had her suit dry cleaned so it would be immaculate. She was ready.

Case Study

What a hefty tax return! Scott test drove a new car. He realized the ride was almost as smooth as his current car, which was running fine. While a new car would be fun he decided that being out of debt would be better and socked the cash into paying off his mortgage.

Case Study

The apartment had been fine for two people, but now that there was a baby and a dog it was a different story! Even though they regularly de-cluttered and loved the low rent payment, they were bursting at the seams. The frustration of the current situation was not healthy. They didn't need a mansion, but it was definitely time for more space!

Fast Track ReflACTION

1) In what ways should you spend more time, energy, and money on improving appearance?

_____

_____

_____

2) In what ways should you spend less time, energy, and money on appearance?

_____

_____

_____

3) How does an awareness of anxiety and reasonable decisions increase your effectiveness and overall enjoyment of life? What changes would be beneficial? (Try them.)

_____

_____

_____

Journal Insights

Write insights regarding the chapter contents. Insights might include how these concepts affect you: is power given to others through appearance worries; returns on time, money, energy investment; are reasonable choices easy; is worth tied to appearance.

_____

_____

_____

_____

_____

_____

_____

Test Yourself

    A. True power comes from abandoning what?

_____

_____

    B. Name three things specifically mentioned as appearance tools.

_____

_____

    C. It's time to "rethink" things if appearance anxiety comes at the expense of what four things?

_____

_____

    D. Name the five primary needs.

_____

_____

    E. Markets perpetuate indefinitely when markets can appear to meet _____ _____; worth is attached to _____? This can result in styles (and performances) which are well-done _____.

_____

_____

20. Emo Safety
Securing

Empower Yourself
Emotionally wacky, or…emotionally savvy.

Summary
- Ability to maintain emotional safety is emotional IQ, and it's the greatest overall predictor of success.
- Emotional safety is not optional. It includes feeling secure, respected, appreciated, loved, confident, and capable.
- People get wacky without emotional safety. Losing it hurts.
- Emotional wounds are real.
- Worry doesn't change vulnerability performing. Performance fear usually involves emotional safety.
- There are two ways to get emotional safety: manipulation and respect.
- Performance manipulation is trying to persuade audience approval through a good enough performance.
- Artistry is skillfully giving a gift to others; manipulation is seeking something from others (like esteem, praise, etc.)

- Manipulation can surface in underhanded maltreatment, crafty maneuvering, or kindness with strings attached.
- Kind manipulation is damaging to giver and receiver, there's unexpressed expectations. Genuine kindness is being kind because that's who you are, no reciprocal strings expected.
- Genuine people can pop up in unexpected places and they make great friends. Being a genuine person increases emotional safety and produces a strong core.

Case Study

Alison left the building, shut the door, and leaned on it. Her heart pounded as tears tugged at the corners of her eyes. She felt eaten alive and wondered if she had what it took. The elderly janitor was outside sweeping. She'd seen him before but hadn't paid attention. He glanced at her and spoke as he continued sweeping, "It can be tough, can't it? Take a break and then go back in. I've seen a lot come and go, and you've got what it takes. Don't let the competition get to you." Alison looked over at him through different eyes as she gathered herself and considered his words. He had nothing to gain by being kind to her, but his kindness meant a lot. After that day they occasionally chatted during breaks and became friends. She even brought his favorite doughnut now and then.

Case Study

Anger was rising, accusations were flying, and the production meeting was getting out of hand. Jem stepped back, took a deep breath, and calmly asked everyone to sit down. She waited until she had everyone's attention and then took charge, "I know that we're under a tight deadline and there are some problems, but if you want to speak, it will be done one at a time and with respect. We are still a team, and we need to work together to find a way to meet everyone's needs and make the deadlines."

Case Study

As the branch director, Shelly bent over backwards so the company could move solidly into the next phase. But then the bosses dismantled her work with decisions that contradicted their earlier instructions. This confused clients, doubled her workload, and tightened deadlines. The problem had happened before, and she had hinted at how damaging it was. These people were great to work with other than this problem. If she took the slack another round, would they fix this and be more responsive? Oh wait. Stop. She realized she was manipulating them with kindness and ambiguous expectations. They were also manipulating her by being kind on the outside but not taking responsibility as the unaddressed issues grew and requests fell on deaf ears. Irritation was beginning to surface both ways. It was time to stop manipulating and address the problem directly. Things could not continue as they were without significant damage.

Fast Track ReflACTION

1) In what ways do you seek emotional safety? How can you increase emotional IQ?

_____

_____

_____

2) How does wanting something from someone change the relationship; when have you manipulated and not realized it?

_____

_____

_____

3) Who are your genuine friends; are you a genuine friend?

_____

_____

_____

Journal Insights

Write insights regarding the chapter contents. Insights might include how these concepts affect you: quick fixes seen or used, what emotional wounds are/have you grappled with, influences on emotional safety.

_____

_____

_____

_____

_____

_____

_____

Test Yourself
A. Why isn't manipulation addressed and what does it take to address it?

_____

_____

B. If being "good enough" doesn't work, manipulation might surface in putting what people down; list the five examples given.

_____

_____

C. Name five of the possible ways listed that people get wacky when they don't feel emotionally safe.

_____

_____

D. Outcome anxiety is common because the fear isn't about a performance or outcome. What's at stake?

_____

_____

E. What's the difference between artistry and manipulation?

_____

_____

21. Intrinsic vs. Extrinsic Worth
Claiming

Empower Yourself
Constantly climb, or…automatically shine.

Summary
- There are two types of self-worth: intrinsic and extrinsic.
- Intrinsic worth is based on internal worth as a human being. This invites personal bests and mutual support.
- Extrinsic worth is based on rank and comparisons. This results in continual competitiveness for security.
- The difference is not honors but *comparisons.* A person can have intrinsic worth and receive honors.
- Society is built on pursuing extrinsic worth. Most agree that intrinsic worth is best, but fears and fallacies preclude it.
- Extrinsic worth is unstable as others climb to the top to supplant.
- Research strongly supports the value of intrinsic worth.
- Intrinsic worth is obtained by abandoning comparisons and focusing on self-improvement. Genuine value of self and others can be felt.
- Intrinsic worth is a choice.

Case Study

Lori was being taped in front of a live audience for an internationally broadcast TV special comprised of celebrities. In the middle of her solo her microphone caught feedback. In a single smooth movement, she instinctively changed body direction, extended the mic away, and lowered her volume. But these split-second, professional responses didn't correct the problem. So, without skipping a second beat, she delightfully chimed, "Sing mic! Sing!" and continued. The potentially embarrassing moment immediately turned to laughter and warmth. It was just enough time for the sound engineer to correct the problem, and the performance continued without a hitch. It didn't matter that future audiences would see the replays; their reaction would be the same as the live one.

Case Study

Angie called her mom. "I just don't think I can do it. I'm ready to drop out of the program." She explained how fear gripped her every time she had to present for a professor, yet presenting would be a big part of this career if she finished her degree. "My mind races or blanks and I feel stupid." Her mom listened and finally said, "Angie, is it that you don't like this career or that you don't like anxiety?" If you like the career, go for it and figure the anxiety out. Honestly, if you're this worried about what they think that fear could follow you into another career. At some point you'll have to determine you are valued regardless of how a presentation turns out. Truly feeling that will help your mind settle."

Case Study

A new university professor stepped up to perform a cello solo at a community benefit. The program was composed of top musicians to whom he would naturally be compared. He took stage, carefully placed his music, and soon virtuoso cello music filled the hall. All went well until he reached to gently pull down some music pages when they all tumbled. What did he do? Loud and strong he sang his part with a wide grin as he scooped up the music. Then he resumed and continued beautifully to the end. The audience applauded wildly, more than for any other performer yet he had the most obvious error. In the moment of uncertainty, intrinsic worth pulled him through and the audience response was delight and admiration.

Fast Track ReflACTION

1) Do you operate from a perspective of intrinsic or extrinsic worth; when; why? (Consider comparisons.)

---

2) What might hamper your sense of intrinsic worth? (Consider social and personal influences.)

_____

_____

_____

3) What advantages might be experienced from a consistent focus on intrinsic worth?

_____

_____

_____

Journal Insights

Write insights regarding the chapter contents. Insights might include how these concepts affect you: effect of comparisons, security, intrinsic vs. extrinsic behavior; how a more intrinsic focus could be of benefit.

_____

_____

_____

_____

_____

_____

_____

_____

Test Yourself

A. Extrinsic worth isn't from achievement; extrinsic worth is measured by _____; intrinsic worth comes from _____. Extrinsic worth _____ ability; intrinsic worth _____ ability.

_____

_____

B. Write two of the questions that can be asked to determine reliance on intrinsic vs. extrinsic worth.

_____

_____

C. In reality, research shows that those with intrinsic worth have deeper what? Name the five things.

_____

_____

D. You can't predict what will happen in a _____ so you just _____.

_____

_____

E. [When there's intrinsic worth] since each person is _____, energy need not be diverted to_____; so there are more resources available for _____ and _____.

_____

_____

22. THE Best vs. MY Best
Enjoying

Empower Yourself
The best, or…my best.

Summary

- There are two mindsets: "the best" and "my best."
- "The best" focuses on recognition, awards, categories sub-categories.
- Competitions or losing isn't the problem. Extrinsic focus is the problem.
- "The best" switches attention from patience, process, and progress to pride, pursuit, and put downs. Effort and true growth are shortchanged.
- Competition can drive people to damage themselves or others, "I'm better because I can hurt myself" or "I'm better because I can hurt you."
- A "the best" mentality implies that worth must be earned.
- Any time a person engages in extrinsic worth, self and others are damaged to some degree.
- Extrinsic worth indicates a need for greater core power.
- "My best" is a better mentality. "My best" is consistent, diligent focus on self-improvement regardless of rank.

- "The best" is exclusive, cutthroat, damaging to relationships, detrimental and demanding. "My best" is inclusive, cooperative, supportive of relationships, delightful, and deliberate.
- The distinction is *how* and *why* honors are sought. Honors aren't bad, but achieving them to prove self-worth is damaging.
- "My best" can't be faked. It's achieved instantly by shifting focus.
- Top athletes are usually grounded in "my best", which gives them an edge. A major benefit of "my best" is to unlock highest potential.

Case Study

Mae always wanted to take ballet, but her family couldn't afford it. Now she longingly watched her daughter's lessons. One day she asked herself why she didn't just start! Sure it would take years to become proficient, but she could wait inside the class as easily as outside. The next week she squeezed into a leotard, told her daughter to suck up any embarrassment (it couldn't be worse than her own), gathered courage, and joined. She ignored the stares from the kids and other moms and just did her best. After the initial adjustment, it wasn't so bad. In fact, it was fun! In time Mae's waistline shrank, muscles took shape, and confidence soared. She said, "Kids don't get to have all the fun. Adults can grow."

Case Study

A student said, "I stopped comparing myself with others and just worked. I decided to be my best in private." Prior to this she won most competitions; afterwards, she was unstoppable. Ironically, she said that when her attitude changed, winning competitions didn't mean as much to her. Instead she loved seeing how far she could push herself. *That's* the difference between "the best" and "my best."

Case Study

The director of a children's theater company returned from a vacation to New York. She commented to a staff member that doing a show on Broadway was a piece of cake. The friend asked why. She pointed to several names in the Broadway program and said, "I do the jobs of all these people. I direct, do most of the tech, and manage all the publicity! We're not Broadway, but we don't have to be the best to make a difference and change kids' lives!"

Fast Track ReflACTION
1) List advantages and disadvantages of "the best" and "my best"? How can abandoning comparisons and rank increase success?

2) Have you seen or experienced these things: "I'm better because I can hurt myself" or "I'm better because I can hurt you?" What are the long-term effects? Should you get help to overcome one of these?

_____

_____

_____

3) In what ways do pride, pursuit, and put downs hurt you? In what ways can increasing (or encouraging) patience, process, and progress help you? (Try it.)

_____

_____

_____

Journal Insights

Write insights regarding the chapter contents. Insights might include how these concepts affect you: analyzing competitors in a "the best" or "my best" mind state and how it affects preparation and competition, ability to feel worth without comparisons, core strength.

_____

_____

_____

_____

_____

_____

_____

Test Yourself

A. A "the best" mentality shifts focus from what three things to what three things.

_____

_____

B. A "the best" mentality is damaging regardless of whether an individual is winning or losing; list the five reasons.

_____

_____

C. Honors aren't the problem. It's the _____ and _____ focus. It's _____ and _____ honors are approached and sought. Honors aren't a problem, but achieving them to _____ is.

_____

_____

D. How many can simultaneously be "the best", how many can simultaneously be "my best."

_____

_____

E. "My best" can't be faked. If a person tries _____ to be _____ it doesn't work because there are still _____. The focus must be absolutely and completely on _____.

_____

_____

23. Subtle Bullying
Spotting

Empower Yourself
Bully ignore, or…address and soar.

Summary

- Subtle bullying is a form of manipulation. It affects emotional safety and performance outcomes. It's putting someone down to build self up.
- Subtle group emotional abuse is when individuals unconsciously (or consciously) band together to put someone down or pressure them.
- A response is "You're too sensitive." But more sensitivity is needed. Bullying causes physical, mental, emotional and behavioral symptoms.
- Abusers say, "I'll walk on you, you will let me; this will prove I'm good." Enablers say, "I'll let you walk on me, in time you will see I'm good and change, and this will prove I'm good." Users say, "I'll try not to walk on you, but if it's inconvenient, I'll indirectly assist or remain silent as you're walked on, and this will keep me looking good." Users are indirect abusers.
- Small physical wounds can be disruptive, so can small emotional wounds, especially if repeated with no recovery time.

- It's painful to recognize that one has been bullied or has bullied. Rather than blame or shame, grow and move on.
- Overt and subtle bullying have the same cause and solution. Gangs and races clash because they are the same—they lack emotional safety. Bullying happens *within* these groups, not just *between* them.
- Subtle bullying must be spotted to be fixed. Doing so reduces anxiety.

Case Study

Sheela was eager to start her first day in this prestigious dance company. It would take a little while to "learn the ropes," but she figured others would understand and help. She jumped in, but it didn't take long to make a minor mistake. As she quickly fixed it, she noticed disapproving looks from the person next to her and covered whispers from two people across the room. Sheela felt a little unsettled and her movements became tenuous. She cleared her thoughts, brushed away the fleeting desire to hide in embarrassment, and resumed her tasks.

Case Study

Karl walked into the locker room. Wow! He couldn't believe he'd made the varsity team! Ard, the varsity captain, openly welcomed him. Then Jim strolled in. Karl and Jim usually walked home together. Ard looked at Jim, rolled his eyes toward other varsity players and they quietly smirked. Karl ignored and warmly responded, "See you guys around!" He waved as he left with Jim. Karl figured he'd first try genuine respect and friendship since Ard seemed decent. If that didn't work, he'd go from there. Other people did not determine his friends. [Karl is using emotional safety and boundaries—which may be increased, if needed. In extreme cases adult intervention may be necessary.]

Case Study

For four years Mara was bullied in elementary school. It started with snubs and snide remarks and escalated to daily spitting and hitting. Parental visits to the teachers, principal, and even higher administration fell on deaf ears. Mara's grades went from the top of the class to the bottom and her extrovert personality became withdrawn. Then she was beaten badly enough it was not certain whether she would lose permanent teeth. She begged not to return the last three weeks of the year. Her parents agreed and then moved in the summer. At the new school Mara's grades were back up within weeks. [This story includes both subtle and overt bullying. It is used to illustrate how bullying affects ability and personality. When leaders failed to intervene the problem slowly escalated from subtle bulling, snubbing, and snide remarks to overt bullying and serious injuries.]

Fast Track ReflACTION
1) When have you seen/experienced subtle bullying; name the physical, mental, emotional, and/or behavioral symptoms?

_____

_____

_____

2) Have you subtly abused, enabled, or used? If so, when, why? (Consider emotional safety.) What positive things could result from healthier interaction?

_____

_____

_____

3) How can spotting subtle bullying (especially in the moment) help prevent or reduce anxiety?

_____

_____

_____

Journal Insights

Write insights regarding the chapter contents. Insights might include how these concepts affect you: experiencing or engaging in subtle bullying, reasons, ways to handle situations appropriately, resources to address it.

_____

_____

_____

_____

_____

_____

Test Yourself

   A. The person bullied may struggle with what two things?

_____

_____

   B. The person bullying may be at a loss to do what?

_____

_____

   C. What happens if a leader in an organization ignores or joins subtle bullying?

_____

_____

   D. Overt and subtle bullying between people in a group and between groups is because people are the same—they lack_____. It's the _____ problem and the only _____.

_____

_____

   E. Group emotional abuse solicitation can happen through what kinds of body language. Name five things.

_____

_____

24. Choose Respect
Protecting

Empower Yourself
Endlessly maneuver, or…always respect.

Summary
- Boundaries are a protective fence so tasks can be attended to.
- Boundaries are probably the most important performance skill.
- Whenever there is outcome anxiety there is a boundary problem.
- A chooser says, "I won't walk on you and you won't walk on me." Choosers expect respect even if they mess up, and give respect even if others mess up.
- Abusers disrespect others; enablers disrespect self.
- Boundaries are common in society and appropriate in personal life.
- Boundaries provide emotional safety. Boundaries are a substitute for respect and eliminate the need for manipulation.
- The quality of a person's boundaries is reflected in their relationships and personal safety.

- There are defining characteristics between boundaries and manipulation. Boundaries are if/then statements that are respectful and firm
- Mental boundaries dramatically strengthen the inner core; they are like putting on armor. Worry happens when unsafe; boundaries are safe.
- Respect is given freely; trust is given conditionally. Earned trust and selective boundaries protect better than manipulation.
- Disagreement does not equal disrespect.
- A person who gives respect can more easily expect it; a person who expects respect can more easily give it.
- Choosers use boundaries and give and expect respect 100% of the time. (Except in abusive situations involving extreme physical danger, see Appendix B in *Boost Core Power and Bust Anxiety.*)

Case Study

Sheela (from the last chapter) limited interactions with those who were unkind. She finished her year contract with the internationally acclaimed dance company and then chose to leave. She said, "I didn't like the daily cat fights. I traded the prestige of being in the chorus of that company with the prestige of being a principle dancer in my regional company. I'm happier." [Boundary: *if* you are unkind, *then* my relationship with you will be strictly professional; and, *if* I am not treated with respect, *then* I will not dance for you.]

Case Study

Angelina could not wait to meet her friend for lunch. "You know how you suggested using a mental boundary with my new boss because of his arrogance about the promotion? It's been very helpful! I can get work done without fuming. When he's that way I just think, 'If you're respectful to me then I will value your friendship, and if you're not I won't. Either way, I will do my job well because that's the kind of person I am.' Since doing this I'm not frustrated any more. In fact, he might be doing it because he's insecure. I hadn't considered that before." [Boundaries create safety; safety increases brain function and deepens awareness.]

Case Study

Jed was surprised when his manager burst in. She ranted on about him not fulfilling his responsibilities. He calmly waited and then responded, "No one told me of this policy change. If you don't inform me then I can't make the change. If you will email me a copy of the new policies I will read it and make the necessary changes." [When he calmly waited, he did two things. He avoided quick-fix responses and shut down brains that would have made the situation messy, and he implemented the mental boundary, "I refuse to take responsibility for your mistakes." He then implemented a verbal boundary which essentially said, "If you let me know, then I will do it; if you don't, then I can't and won't." By remaining calm, he showed her respect; by setting mental and verbal boundaries, he expected respect.]

Fast Track ReflACTION

1) Why should respect be unconditional, while trust and boundaries are conditional? How does each protect?

_____

_____

_____

2) If a person deserves less respect when messing up, how does this negatively impact you or others even if no mistakes are made?

_____

_____

_____

3) Think of a situation that you could improve by expecting or giving more respect; what if/then boundary could help?

_____

_____

_____

Journal Insights

Write insights regarding the chapter contents. Insights might include how these concepts affect you: when do you use manipulative quick fixes or boundaries, what mental boundaries would be helpful, how core safety affects anxiety.

_____

_____

_____

_____

_____

_____

Test Yourself

   A. In a performance the performer has relationships with the audience in what two possible ways?

_____

_____

   B. List five characteristics of boundaries and five characteristics of manipulation from the chart.

_____

_____

   C. When there's _____, a _____ is needed; a boundary is a substitute for _____.

_____

_____

   D. Manipulation is perpetuated by the fallacy that _____.

_____

_____

   E. There are two ways to get emotional safety, what are they? (One provides safety, the other only pseudo safety.)

_____

_____

25. Strong and Squeaky Clean
Responding

Empower Yourself
Messy manipulation, or…boundaries and responsibility.

Summary
- Most fear is a lack of core power. Core power requires boundaries and cleaning your side of the street. Manipulation of self, others or environment is a quick fix attempt to grasp emotional safety.
- There's never a loss of focus, and two types of focus: self-consciousness and self-awareness. Self-consciousness is addressed by boundaries.
- Negative self-talk is a form of emotional abuse. Self-manipulation can be addressed by considering *why the resistance?*
- It's never appropriate to dodge responsibility.
- Emotional pain, relationship problems, and performance problems are usually from manipulation, like subtle enabling and subtle abusing. Manipulation includes attempting to be understood when resisted.
- Respect, boundaries, non-manipulation, responsibility, and integrity provide the ultimate emotional safety, and opportunity for maximum ability. These things melt fear.

Case Study

Dylan prepped for the final play of the game as someone yelled from the stands, "If you miss we lose the championship! This season is on you!" Tension gripped him. He stepped back, took a breath and shot up a mental boundary. *Everyone on the team is responsible for where we are. I am only responsible to do my best.* Core strength surged. He set the ball and let it fly. [Boundary: *If* you are unreasonable or disrespectful, *then* I won't listen. However, I will take responsibility to fulfill my commitments as best I can.]

Case Study

Melba was shocked to be yelled at in the meeting for enforcing the new attendance and work policy. She had done *exactly* what the board agreed on and gave clear explanations to employees prior to enforcement. But some employees complained (who were family members to her superiors.) When accused, Melba explained that the enforcement was impartial and non-punitive expecting this would calm things. But instead they accused her of defending inappropriate behavior! Melba was astonished and at a loss to solve the problem. Later she realized that though employees significantly manipulated the board and the board significantly manipulated her; and though she had not manipulated the employees, she *did* manipulate the board by seeking understanding. When she took responsibility for her part answers came. Next time she'd simply say, "I was carrying out your request. If that's not what you wanted, what do you want?" Then the responsibility to solve the problem would be squarely placed on the shoulders of those who caused the problem.

Case Study

Annette extended kindness to less advantaged people. She gave the benefit of the doubt until she heard jokes behind her back. Despite wanting to help others, she would not interact with or provide opportunities to those who were not respectful. [Boundary: "*If* I'm respected, *then* I'd love to help; *if* I'm not respected, *then* I won't." If she tried to *change* them (especially for recognition, appreciation or emotional safety) or punish (whether successful or not), then her action would be manipulation despite that it was in the form of an if/then boundary. Only she could know her true intent (and intent can change). Other's judgments of her— accurate or inaccurate were conjecture. If she attempted to correct inaccurate conjecture, they resisted and she persisted, it would be manipulation even if her motive was to re-establish assistance.]

Fast Track ReflACTION

1) Name a recent internal self-manipulation; answer *why the resistance*? (Consider deeply any possible reasons for resistance.)

2) Name a recent time in which you were manipulated; what boundary would provide a good response? (Try it. Remember, a boundary that isn't strong enough doesn't protect; a boundary that's punitively strong is manipulation.)

_____

_____

_____

3) Name a recent time in which you manipulated someone; what boundary would be better? (Try it. Consider audiences or associates; doing well or looking good enough; and boundaries and intrinsic worth.)

_____

_____

_____

Journal Insights

Write insights regarding the chapter contents. Insights might include how these concepts affect you: self-awareness vs. self-consciousness, imposter syndrome, level of proactive safety, quality of self-talk, need to be understood when misjudged, interpersonal skills to improve performance ability.

_____

_____

_____

_____

_____

_____

Test Yourself

A. There are two types of focus, what are they? _____ which is associated with these positive things (name five from the list) and _____ which is associated with these negative things (name five from the list).

_____

_____

B. The same action could be an appropriate boundary or inappropriate manipulation depending on what?

_____

_____

C. Proactive self-improvement requires proactive _____? Admitting a _____ is like a rickety bridge; it feels _____ and _____; if not stabilized by _____, manipulation and _____ take over to increase safety.

_____

_____

D. Boundaries protect interpersonally, but failed attempts to improve can lead to _____....which can lead to negative self-care. _____, _____, and _____ can cause life to become _____. These weaken the _____.

_____

_____

E. Cleaning your side of the street is a_____ deal. (Name the four things.) Admitting faults can be hard, especially if _____ (name the two things).

_____

_____

26. Fail...and Other Smart Things
Rebounding

Empower Yourself
Work harder, or...work smarter.

Summary
- "Deliberate failing" determinates current skills and speeds progress.
- "Never perform always practice" focuses effort and reduces pressure.
- "Telling Stories" overrides natural negative safety mechanisms.
- "Recovered perfectionist" combats not being good enough.
- "Take it down a notch" reduces emotion to improve brain function.
- "Challenge, counter, credit" combats negative self-talk.
- "Balance" improves performance through a well-rounded approach.
- "Everything" is a way to ensure life awareness.
- "No benefits please" reduces omitting desirable things.
- "Don't be so responsible" prevents over-responsibility or enabling.
- "Abandon embarrassment" shifts shame to respect/responsibility/goals.
- Lower expectations" decreases pressure by changing expectations.
- "Never lose" increases learning in every situation

- "Reverse procrastination" keeps pressure low and brain function up.
- "Time to time" reduces drag and increases motivation and fun.
- "Work don't worry" postpones worry so the work can be completed.
- "My best rewards club" increases success through structure and praise.
- "Five seconds to success" adjusts initial effort to one's favor.
- "Enslave yourself" uses neuroplasticity aggressively.
- "Go play" deliberately increases rejuvenation.
- "Be selfish" positively supports self while respecting others.

Case Study

RaNae looked at the work list and felt overwhelmed. But she knew better than to let apprehension sink in. Out came her stopwatch app and the race was on! She triumphantly checked off items. By going at lightning speed she not only moved her forward faster, her mind was more clear. The last item on the list wasn't due until next week. It was almost time to go but she knew that sticking it out could make a big difference. She broke the task into sections, tackled the first small section, checked it off, and left work on time. She was the champion of the work list! Wahoooo, cheers, applause! She took a victory lap down the hall and out the building! Now to go home and play...

Case Study

At dinner Melinda told her husband that in practice she'd set the metronome extra fast to test her limit; she started working just lower than the speed she failed. Her husband laughed and said he did the same type of thing with the weight machine at the gym; he found where he couldn't lift, went down a weight and started the workout.

Cast Study

Mischee was in a minor accident and unable to do anything for her husband's birthday. On top of that, he was out of town and on a diet. The initial story in her head was that it was awful that her injury prevented doing something special before he left, that it was sad he was alone on his birthday, and that they couldn't even do something fun when he returned because of the diet. But then she changed the story. Without the accident they wouldn't have shared all the sweet moments as he tenderly helped her. He now had well-earned quality time for himself, and a trim waistline was a hundred times better than a piece of cake!

Fast Track ReflACTION

1) How could you increase your success by routinely planning to fail; how can changing your stories help? (Try it.)

_____

_____

_____

2) Which of the anti-procrastination skills could be most fun and beneficial to you; why? (Try it.)

_____

_____

_____

3) Which of your three "everything" areas need the most attention, what other skill/s listed may help you improve it; what might be the benefits? (Try it.)

_____

_____

_____

Journal Insights

Write insights regarding the chapter contents. Insights might include how these concepts affect you: when do you feel drag, why; what core skills could empower; what skills could help in multiple situations or help overcome negative patterns.

_____

_____

_____

_____

_____

_____

_____

_____

Test Yourself

A. What three things are involved in the "everything" test?

_____

_____

B. Expectations are premeditated _____; do _____ instead?

_____

_____

C. High emotion _____ the thinking parts of the brain. Taking emotion down just one notch avoids both _____ and _____.

_____

_____

D. Pushing forward without considering feelings is likely to _____ and _____?

_____

_____

E. The reason to check stories is because _____ create _____ which affect _____? So monitor _____.

_____

_____

27. Core Integrity
Encouraging

Empower Yourself
Reactive control, or…proactive integrity.

Summary
- Peak flow in the zone is not the Mount Everest of performance; core integrity is. Core integrity isn't optimal performing; it's optimal *being*.
- Core integrity requires going deep enough to truly understand. Integrity changes you. Control muddies understanding and limits ability.
- A clear focus on the core self unlocks an internal power that flows to you without compulsion. Core integrity can't be faked.
- Self-love and self-value can become abundant without effort. Core integrity radiates from the inside out. Every person has access to the power of core integrity; it's there for the taking.
- Core integrity focuses thinking.
- Knowledge unlocks ability and supplies sustainability and stability; a solid core provides internal strength in all stages of life.

- Core integrity is a lifetime pursuit. Fear melts when there's understanding. Core integrity is a rock-solid gift you give yourself.
- Core integrity yields emotional safety, awesome brain function, increased performance ability, improved relationships, deep respect, and intrinsic worth. When you have it…you *know*.

Case Study

A guest pianist, Marvin Goldstein, traveled across the nation to play for an enthusiastic, packed crowd in a huge university theater in California. The crowd cheered and clamored for encore after encore. The next night, he donated a free concert in another community. Though extensively advertised, the hall was empty except two people and one family who had driven a distance to see both concerts. The nearly empty building seemed cavernous and the attendees wondered if the concert would be canceled or cut short. At the appointed time, Mr. Goldstein stood in his tuxedo and eagerly said, "Oh good! This means we can get to know each other! Come on stage where it's easier to see!" His virtuoso concert rivaled the night before, but also included personal touches. He addressed each person by name. He used their phone numbers as melodies in complicated improvisations and effortlessly combined their favorite songs into hilarious musical arrangements. Afterward, the children got an autographed picture. It provided inspiration as they became skilled musicians. Why were both concerts powerful? Core integrity.

Case Study

Claudia's patience was justifiably thin. She had requested that the maintenance crew not change the location of items, but it was still happening. She knew that storming around might result in a temporary fix, but in the end it would just shut down brains and not internally motivate. Instead of anger, she used a boundary. When they came for their pay she simply said they could have it when items were replaced correctly and if it happened again, pay would be deducted for her supervisory time. Increasing core integrity meant she took more responsibility to communicate and use boundaries rather than use quick fix anger. She stopped trying to control and let them decide how to respond.

Case Study

Joe's increased effort at team practice backfired. He was so frustrated he felt like "spitting nails" but instead he stepped back, took a deep breath and thought, "Okay, let's get real. I'm trying to use control of this ball to control the perceptions of my coach and team mates. *No more control!* Just feel the energy of the movement and enjoy deep awareness of muscles, mood, and mindfulness." He released control and things started to click again.

Fast Track ReflACTION
1) Why is ultimate *being* more important than ultimate performance?

_____

_____

_____

2) Why does abandoning control provide more "control"?

_____

_____

_____

3) What obstacles stand in the way of having core integrity; what benefits might be experienced from addressing obstacles?

_____

_____

_____

Journal Insights

Write insights regarding the chapter contents. Insights might include how these concepts affect you: rock-solid emotional safety, fake integrity, how to deepen core power, why core power eliminates anxiety, how releasing control creates more power.

_____

_____

_____

_____

_____

_____

_____

Test Yourself

    A. The gap between your current self and better self can be felt. Growth is *not* _____? Name the four things listed.

_____

_____

    B. Core integrity is a lifetime pursuit and a rock-solid gift given to self that provides what? Name the five things listed.

_____

_____

    C. Control assumes that something needs to be _____ into _____ or _____. This is _____.

_____

_____

    D. Why are most core concerns ignored instead of explored?

_____

_____

    E. Real core power comes from _____ _____ _____. If it's lost, it is regained by _____.

_____

_____

28. Effective Leadership
Lifting

Empower Yourself
Reasonably instructive, or…amazingly effective.

Summary
- Anxiety management and consistent peak flow/zone are developable skills. This isn't pandering, wasting time, or reducing expectations.
- Dedicated leaders deserve praise for helpful anxiety information.
- It took time for seemingly unrelated fields to combine inventions.
- The importance of anxiety management was not initially understood.
- Anxiety weeds people out of a field, causing a possible "teaching gap."
- Leaders can feel incapable of successfully handling situations. Stressful anxiety literally *burns out* energy. Anxiety management reduces burnout.
- Often leaders are already doing some anxiety management. Knowledge maximizes potential benefits.
- Certain questions can immediately reduce anxiety.
- Fear is contagious. It can be countered.

- Common leadership methods increase anxiety—like reward systems.
- Trust increases the ability to improve. Reducing student burnout reduces teacher burnout.

Case Study

These two situations were about five years apart. One was before I studied anxiety, the other after. These students were advanced high school piano students with similar personalities and preparation. A nationally certified adjudicator was sent from the state teachers' association to judge them on the exact same material.

At lesson, I asked the first student if she wanted to do the adjudication. She said yes. I asked why she stopped practicing. She averted her eyes and said she didn't know. She was overwhelmed, embarrassed and ashamed. I was exasperated and out of ideas. (Notice *my* anxiety?) I strongly encouraged practice and proceeded to help her stumble through as best I could. It was painful for both of us. She did not pass the adjudication and soon dropped out. I thought the situation was primarily due to her lack of preparation...until the second student.

At lesson, I asked him if he wanted to do the adjudication. He said yes. I asked why he stopped practicing. He averted his eyes and said he didn't know. He was overwhelmed, embarrassed and ashamed. I said, "I think I know why." He turned his lowered head to peer at me, expecting the worst. I said, "It's just a little performance anxiety." (Of course it was a lot of anxiety, but I was using recommended anxiety management intervention.)

I asked, "Do you feel capable of successfully handling this situation?" He said, "*NO!*" surprising even himself at the strength of his emotion. I said, "That's what I thought. But it's really no big deal. Research shows that ability is usually higher than it seems and that things improve immediately when anxiety is addressed. You think you're miles from success but you're probably only inches." I asked him to play the first scale. It was a *mess.* (I honestly didn't think he could pass, but I put trust in the research.) I said, "What was wrong with the scale?" He said, "Everything!"

I said, "Really? Let's see." He played again. It was still a *mess,* but he noticed a thumb cross problem and commented on it. (My reactions reduced his anxiety enough for his brain to work.) I said, "Okay, everything else can be wrong but not that cross." He played with 100% accuracy. It was slower than required, but accurate. I was shocked.

I summoned all my acting ability and smiled as if I expected this, "See, you're closer than you think." I explained anxiety and that it's easier to play with the brain. We continued. I interjected anxiety information. I said his procrastination was just anxiety and provided tricks to jump past it. He left invigorated. He practiced harder than ever and passed. He was elated...and so was I.

The story doesn't stop there. I had contact with the first student. I shared anxiety information and apologized for not knowing what to do earlier. After long avoidance, she began dabbling and now teaches music. Anxiety information matters.

Case Study

The coach came over, "You did that well, but there are two things left that will now cement this. First, notice how your brain feels. If there's discomfort keep at it until your thoughts are comfortable. Then, once your thoughts are comfortable deliberately repeat the high quality movement and thought so it becomes second nature and firmly planted in your muscle memory. The idea is: don't do it until you can do it right, do it until it's completely comfortable and you "can't" do it wrong. Awareness of your thoughts will reduce the possibility of anxiety causing problems in the game." [Anxiety management skills strengthen core power.]

Case Study

Mark heard complaints about his leadership behind his back. He reached out in a sincere attempt to resolve the situation. But his emails and phone messages were not reciprocated, let alone suggestions made to mutually solve problems. He made another attempt. When there was still no response it was now a reflection on them; it took both sides for a solution. They either did not have the desire or the skills to resolve the situation. He would leave the door open to resolving things; however, if they continued to undermine he would use boundaries and document information to protect himself.

Fast Track ReflACTION

1) How can you reduce stress and burnout as a leader?

_____

_____

_____

2) What clarifications regarding rules, expectations, consequences, and support could empower you and those you lead? Are you consistent and fair?

_____

_____

_____

3) What challenging things give you anxiety and/or empathy?

_____

_____

_____

Journal Insights

Write insights regarding the chapter contents. Insights might include how these concepts affect you: burnout in self and others, current anxiety strategies, helpful things to try, ways to better support self and others.

_____

_____

_____

_____

_____

_____

_____

_____

Test Yourself

A. Personalities change depending on which person?

_____

_____

B. Fear is contagious. It can _____ in a _____, _____ or _____. Heading it off _____.

_____

_____

C. The most common factor in underachievement is _____. It's the underlying cause of _____ (list four).

_____

_____

D. Leaders don't just supervise skill execution. They establish _____.

_____

_____

E. Those who don't have anxiety must work as hard to _____ as those with anxiety have to work to _____?

_____

_____

Section II.
Increase Ability

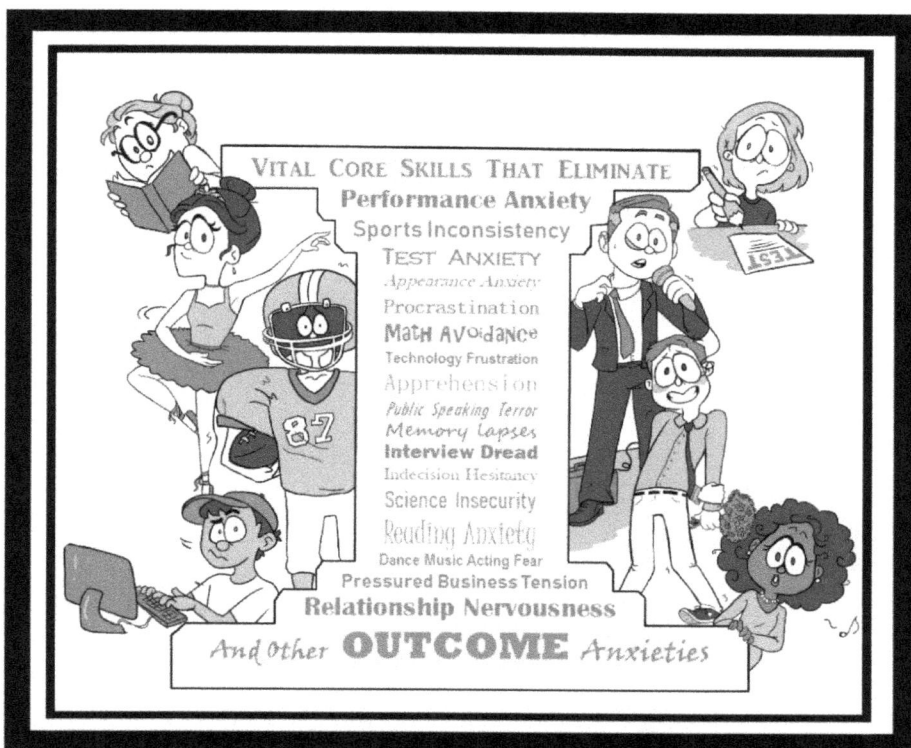

VITAL CORE SKILLS THAT ELIMINATE
Performance Anxiety
Sports Inconsistency
TEST ANXIETY
Appearance Anxiety
Procrastination
Math Avoidance
Technology Frustration
Apprehension
Public Speaking Terror
Memory Lapses
Interview Dread
Indecision Hesitancy
Science Insecurity
Reading Anxiety
Dance Music Acting Fear
Pressured Business Tension
Relationship Nervousness
And Other OUTCOME *Anxieties*

Building core ability through directed observations during practice and performance.

Section II is designed to build core strength through the application of core concepts. It consists of four six-week application phases and space to write observations. Phases can be done simultaneously with Section I or independently, back to back, or as needed. It is recommended that at least one full phase is completed

Propel Progress
To systematically evaluate practice and performance
To practice anxiety management prior to performance
To evaluate performance skill development
To set goals within a systematic framework
To develop emotional IQ skills

Phase I.

Propel Progress

Application

A

Increase Ability
Building core ability through directed observations
during practice and performance.

Notice thoughts and feelings.
Notice influences affecting ability.
Set realistic but challenging goals every time.
Always evaluate whether the goal was achieved.
Build sequentially on past goals and achievements.
If ability changes, *something* changed; find out why.

Core Power Pro-Launch Pad:
Propel Progress 1

Practice or performance (circle one)   **Date:**

TYPE of performance (circle) Tests/Sports/Business/Performing Arts/Other:

Observed problem/s:

Yes/No **Last goal completed?** (circle)

Type of Goal: (circle) Performance Ability/Emotional IQ/Life Balance/Respect self/Respect Others/No manipulation/Take Responsibility/Other:

Goal/s:

Observations	Notes
What happens	
When	
Where	
Why	
How Much	

OBSERVATIONS	Circle	Practice Performance (circle)
Worst ever quality	1 2 3 4 5 6 7 8 9 10	Awesome over-all quality
Incapacitating anxiety, Totally unsure	1 2 3 4 5 6 7 8 9 10	Great flow/zone, Totally sure
Focus on THE Best/compare/Extrinsic	1 2 3 4 5 6 7 8 9 10	Focus on MY Best/share/Intrinsic
Totally degraded others	1 2 3 4 5 6 7 8 9 10	Totally respected others
Totally belittled self	1 2 3 4 5 6 7 8 9 10	Totally respected self
Nada zip zero preparation/progress	1 2 3 4 5 6 7 8 9 10	Amazing preparation/progress
Total manipulation of others	1 2 3 4 5 6 7 8 9 10	No manipulation of others
Awful. Hated it. Grudges dragging	1 2 3 4 5 6 7 8 9 10	Great! Fun! No inner reservations. Flow/Zone

REFLECTIONS	Comments
Thoughts/feelings effecting output	
Possible cause of positive/negative changes	
Patterns or helpful observations	
Input from leader/mentor/friend	
Insights:	

Name _____ Cl _____

Core Power Pro-Launch Pad:
Propel Progress 2

Practice or performance (circle one)	**Date:**

TYPE of performance (circle) Tests/Sports/Business/Performing Arts/Other:

Observed problem/s:

Last goal completed? (circle)
Yes/No

Type of Goal: (circle) Performance Ability/Emotional IQ/Life Balance/Respect self/Respect Others/No manipulation/Take Responsibility/Other:

Goal/s:

Observations	Notes
What happens	
When	
Where	
Why	
How Much	

OBSERVATIONS	Circle	Practice Performance (circle)
Worst ever quality	1 2 3 4 5 6 7 8 9 10	Awesome over-all quality
Incapacitating anxiety, Totally unsure	1 2 3 4 5 6 7 8 9 10	Great flow/zone, Totally sure
Focus on THE Best/compare/Extrinsic	1 2 3 4 5 6 7 8 9 10	Focus on MY Best/share/Intrinsic
Totally degraded others	1 2 3 4 5 6 7 8 9 10	Totally respected others
Totally belittled self	1 2 3 4 5 6 7 8 9 10	Totally respected self
Nada zip zero preparation/progress	1 2 3 4 5 6 7 8 9 10	Amazing preparation/progress
Total manipulation of others	1 2 3 4 5 6 7 8 9 10	No manipulation of others
Awful. Hated it. Grudges dragging	1 2 3 4 5 6 7 8 9 10	Great! Fun! No inner reservations. Flow/Zone

REFLECTIONS	Comments
Thoughts/feelings effecting output	
Possible cause of positive/negative changes	
Patterns or helpful observations	
Input from leader/mentor/friend	
Insights:	

Name _____ Cl _____

Core Power Pro-Launch Pad:
Propel Progress 3

Practice or performance (circle one)   **Date:**

TYPE of performance (circle) Tests/Sports/Business/Performing Arts/Other:

Observed problem/s:

Last goal completed? (circle)
Yes/No

Type of Goal: (circle) Performance Ability/Emotional IQ/Life Balance/Respect self/Respect Others/No manipulation/Take Responsibility/Other:

Goal/s:

Observations	Notes
What happens	
When	
Where	
Why	
How Much	

OBSERVATIONS	Circle	Practice Performance (circle)
Worst ever quality	1 2 3 4 5 6 7 8 9 10	Awesome over-all quality
Incapacitating anxiety, Totally unsure	1 2 3 4 5 6 7 8 9 10	Great flow/zone, Totally sure
Focus on THE Best/compare/Extrinsic	1 2 3 4 5 6 7 8 9 10	Focus on MY Best/share/Intrinsic
Totally degraded others	1 2 3 4 5 6 7 8 9 10	Totally respected others
Totally belittled self	1 2 3 4 5 6 7 8 9 10	Totally respected self
Nada zip zero preparation/progress	1 2 3 4 5 6 7 8 9 10	Amazing preparation/progress
Total manipulation of others	1 2 3 4 5 6 7 8 9 10	No manipulation of others
Awful. Hated it. Grudges dragging	1 2 3 4 5 6 7 8 9 10	Great! Fun! No inner reservations. Flow/Zone

REFLECTIONS	Comments
Thoughts/feelings effecting output	
Possible cause of positive/negative changes	
Patterns or helpful observations	
Input from leader/mentor/friend	
Insights:	

Name _____ Cl _____

Core Power Pro-Launch Pad:
Propel Progress 4

Practice or performance (circle one)   **Date:**

TYPE of performance (circle) Tests/Sports/Business/Performing Arts/Other:

Observed problem/s:

Last goal completed? (circle)
Yes/No

Type of Goal: (circle) Performance Ability/Emotional IQ/Life Balance/Respect self/Respect Others/No manipulation/Take Responsibility/Other:

Goal/s:

Observations	Notes
What happens	
When	
Where	
Why	
How Much	

OBSERVATIONS	Circle	Practice Performance (circle)
Worst ever quality	1 2 3 4 5 6 7 8 9 10	Awesome over-all quality
Incapacitating anxiety, Totally unsure	1 2 3 4 5 6 7 8 9 10	Great flow/zone, Totally sure
Focus on THE Best/compare/Extrinsic	1 2 3 4 5 6 7 8 9 10	Focus on MY Best/share/Intrinsic
Totally degraded others	1 2 3 4 5 6 7 8 9 10	Totally respected others
Totally belittled self	1 2 3 4 5 6 7 8 9 10	Totally respected self
Nada zip zero preparation/progress	1 2 3 4 5 6 7 8 9 10	Amazing preparation/progress
Total manipulation of others	1 2 3 4 5 6 7 8 9 10	No manipulation of others
Awful. Hated it. Grudges dragging	1 2 3 4 5 6 7 8 9 10	Great! Fun! No inner reservations. Flow/Zone

REFLECTIONS	Comments
Thoughts/feelings effecting output	
Possible cause of positive/negative changes	
Patterns or helpful observations	
Input from leader/mentor/friend	
Insights:	

Name _____ Cl _____

Core Power Pro-Launch Pad:
Propel Progress 5

Practice or performance (circle one)	**Date:**

TYPE of performance (circle) Tests/Sports/Business/Performing Arts/Other:

Observed problem/s:

Last goal completed? (circle)
Yes/No

Type of Goal: (circle) Performance Ability/Emotional IQ/Life Balance/Respect self/Respect Others/No manipulation/Take Responsibility/Other:

Goal/s:

Observations	Notes
What happens	
When	
Where	
Why	
How Much	

CORE POWER PRO-LAUNCH PAD

OBSERVATIONS	Circle	Practice Performance (circle)
Worst ever quality	1 2 3 4 5 6 7 8 9 10	Awesome over-all quality
Incapacitating anxiety, Totally unsure	1 2 3 4 5 6 7 8 9 10	Great flow/zone, Totally sure
Focus on THE Best/compare/Extrinsic	1 2 3 4 5 6 7 8 9 10	Focus on MY Best/share/Intrinsic
Totally degraded others	1 2 3 4 5 6 7 8 9 10	Totally respected others
Totally belittled self	1 2 3 4 5 6 7 8 9 10	Totally respected self
Nada zip zero preparation/progress	1 2 3 4 5 6 7 8 9 10	Amazing preparation/progress
Total manipulation of others	1 2 3 4 5 6 7 8 9 10	No manipulation of others
Awful. Hated it. Grudges dragging	1 2 3 4 5 6 7 8 9 10	Great! Fun! No inner reservations. Flow/Zone

REFLECTIONS	Comments
Thoughts/feelings effecting output	
Possible cause of positive/negative changes	
Patterns or helpful observations	
Input from leader/mentor/friend	
Insights:	

Name _____ Cl _____

Core Power Pro-Launch Pad:
Propel Progress 6

Practice or performance (circle one)　　　　**Date:**

TYPE of performance (circle) Tests/Sports/Business/Performing Arts/Other:

Observed problem/s:

Last goal completed? (circle)
Yes/No

Type of Goal: (circle) Performance Ability/Emotional IQ/Life Balance/Respect self/Respect Others/No manipulation/Take Responsibility/Other:

Goal/s:

Observations	Notes
What happens	
When	
Where	
Why	
How Much	

OBSERVATIONS	Circle	Practice Performance (circle)
Worst ever quality	1 2 3 4 5 6 7 8 9 10	Awesome over-all quality
Incapacitating anxiety, Totally unsure	1 2 3 4 5 6 7 8 9 10	Great flow/zone, Totally sure
Focus on THE Best/compare/Extrinsic	1 2 3 4 5 6 7 8 9 10	Focus on MY Best/share/Intrinsic
Totally degraded others	1 2 3 4 5 6 7 8 9 10	Totally respected others
Totally belittled self	1 2 3 4 5 6 7 8 9 10	Totally respected self
Nada zip zero preparation/progress	1 2 3 4 5 6 7 8 9 10	Amazing preparation/progress
Total manipulation of others	1 2 3 4 5 6 7 8 9 10	No manipulation of others
Awful. Hated it. Grudges dragging	1 2 3 4 5 6 7 8 9 10	Great! Fun! No inner reservations. Flow/Zone

REFLECTIONS	Comments
Thoughts/feelings effecting output	
Possible cause of positive/negative changes	
Patterns or helpful observations	
Input from leader/mentor/friend	
Insights:	

Name _____ Cl _____

Core Power Pro-Launch Pad:
Propel Progress 7

Practice or performance (circle one)	**Date:**

TYPE of performance (circle) Tests/Sports/Business/Performing Arts/Other:

Observed problem/s:

	Last goal completed? (circle)
Yes/No	

Type of Goal: (circle) Performance Ability/Emotional IQ/Life Balance/Respect self/Respect Others/No manipulation/Take Responsibility/Other:

Goal/s:

Observations	Notes
What happens	
When	
Where	
Why	
How Much	

OBSERVATIONS	Circle	Practice Performance (circle)
Worst ever quality	1 2 3 4 5 6 7 8 9 10	Awesome over-all quality
Incapacitating anxiety, Totally unsure	1 2 3 4 5 6 7 8 9 10	Great flow/zone, Totally sure
Focus on THE Best/compare/Extrinsic	1 2 3 4 5 6 7 8 9 10	Focus on MY Best/share/Intrinsic
Totally degraded others	1 2 3 4 5 6 7 8 9 10	Totally respected others
Totally belittled self	1 2 3 4 5 6 7 8 9 10	Totally respected self
Nada zip zero preparation/progress	1 2 3 4 5 6 7 8 9 10	Amazing preparation/progress
Total manipulation of others	1 2 3 4 5 6 7 8 9 10	No manipulation of others
Awful. Hated it. Grudges dragging	1 2 3 4 5 6 7 8 9 10	Great! Fun! No inner reservations. Flow/Zone

REFLECTIONS	Comments
Thoughts/feelings effecting output	
Possible cause of positive/negative changes	
Patterns or helpful observations	
Input from leader/mentor/friend	
Insights:	

Name _____ Cl _____

Core Power Pro-Launch Pad:
Propel Progress 8

Practice or performance (circle one)   **Date:**

TYPE of performance (circle) Tests/Sports/Business/Performing Arts/Other:

Observed problem/s:

Last goal completed? (circle)
Yes/No

Type of Goal: (circle) Performance Ability/Emotional IQ/Life Balance/Respect self/Respect Others/No manipulation/Take Responsibility/Other:

Goal/s:

Observations	Notes
What happens	
When	
Where	
Why	
How Much	

OBSERVATIONS	Circle	Practice Performance (circle)
Worst ever quality	1 2 3 4 5 6 7 8 9 10	Awesome over-all quality
Incapacitating anxiety, Totally unsure	1 2 3 4 5 6 7 8 9 10	Great flow/zone, Totally sure
Focus on THE Best/compare/Extrinsic	1 2 3 4 5 6 7 8 9 10	Focus on MY Best/share/Intrinsic
Totally degraded others	1 2 3 4 5 6 7 8 9 10	Totally respected others
Totally belittled self	1 2 3 4 5 6 7 8 9 10	Totally respected self
Nada zip zero preparation/progress	1 2 3 4 5 6 7 8 9 10	Amazing preparation/progress
Total manipulation of others	1 2 3 4 5 6 7 8 9 10	No manipulation of others
Awful. Hated it. Grudges dragging	1 2 3 4 5 6 7 8 9 10	Great! Fun! No inner reservations. Flow/Zone

REFLECTIONS	Comments
Thoughts/feelings effecting output	
Possible cause of positive/negative changes	
Patterns or helpful observations	
Input from leader/mentor/friend	
Insights:	

Name _____ Cl _____

Core Power Pro-Launch Pad:
Propel Progress 9

Practice or performance (circle one)	**Date:**

TYPE of performance (circle) Tests/Sports/Business/Performing Arts/Other:

Observed problem/s:

Last goal completed? (circle)
Yes/No

Type of Goal: (circle) Performance Ability/Emotional IQ/Life Balance/Respect self/Respect Others/No manipulation/Take Responsibility/Other:

Goal/s:

Observations	Notes
What happens	
When	
Where	
Why	
How Much	

OBSERVATIONS	Circle	Practice Performance (circle)
Worst ever quality	1 2 3 4 5 6 7 8 9 10	Awesome over-all quality
Incapacitating anxiety, Totally unsure	1 2 3 4 5 6 7 8 9 10	Great flow/zone, Totally sure
Focus on THE Best/compare/Extrinsic	1 2 3 4 5 6 7 8 9 10	Focus on MY Best/share/Intrinsic
Totally degraded others	1 2 3 4 5 6 7 8 9 10	Totally respected others
Totally belittled self	1 2 3 4 5 6 7 8 9 10	Totally respected self
Nada zip zero preparation/progress	1 2 3 4 5 6 7 8 9 10	Amazing preparation/progress
Total manipulation of others	1 2 3 4 5 6 7 8 9 10	No manipulation of others
Awful. Hated it. Grudges dragging	1 2 3 4 5 6 7 8 9 10	Great! Fun! No inner reservations. Flow/Zone

REFLECTIONS	Comments
Thoughts/feelings effecting output	
Possible cause of positive/negative changes	
Patterns or helpful observations	
Input from leader/mentor/friend	
Insights:	

Name _____ Cl _____

Core Power Pro-Launch Pad:
Propel Progress 10

Practice or performance (circle one)   **Date:**

TYPE of performance (circle) Tests/Sports/Business/Performing Arts/Other:

Observed problem/s:

Yes/No   **Last goal completed?** (circle)

Type of Goal: (circle) Performance Ability/Emotional IQ/Life Balance/Respect self/Respect Others/No manipulation/Take Responsibility/Other:

Goal/s:

Observations	Notes
What happens	
When	
Where	
Why	
How Much	

OBSERVATIONS	Circle	Practice Performance (circle)
Worst ever quality	1 2 3 4 5 6 7 8 9 10	Awesome over-all quality
Incapacitating anxiety, Totally unsure	1 2 3 4 5 6 7 8 9 10	Great flow/zone, Totally sure
Focus on THE Best/compare/Extrinsic	1 2 3 4 5 6 7 8 9 10	Focus on MY Best/share/Intrinsic
Totally degraded others	1 2 3 4 5 6 7 8 9 10	Totally respected others
Totally belittled self	1 2 3 4 5 6 7 8 9 10	Totally respected self
Nada zip zero preparation/progress	1 2 3 4 5 6 7 8 9 10	Amazing preparation/progress
Total manipulation of others	1 2 3 4 5 6 7 8 9 10	No manipulation of others
Awful. Hated it. Grudges dragging	1 2 3 4 5 6 7 8 9 10	Great! Fun! No inner reservations. Flow/Zone

REFLECTIONS	Comments
Thoughts/feelings effecting output	
Possible cause of positive/negative changes	
Patterns or helpful observations	
Input from leader/mentor/friend	
Insights:	

Name _____ Cl _____

Core Power Pro-Launch Pad:
Propel Progress 11

Practice or performance (circle one)   **Date:**

TYPE of performance (circle) Tests/Sports/Business/Performing Arts/Other:

Observed problem/s:

Last goal completed? (circle)
Yes/No

Type of Goal: (circle) Performance Ability/Emotional IQ/Life Balance/Respect self/Respect Others/No manipulation/Take Responsibility/Other:

Goal/s:

Observations	Notes
What happens	
When	
Where	
Why	
How Much	

OBSERVATIONS	Circle	Practice Performance (circle)
Worst ever quality	1 2 3 4 5 6 7 8 9 10	Awesome over-all quality
Incapacitating anxiety, Totally unsure	1 2 3 4 5 6 7 8 9 10	Great flow/zone, Totally sure
Focus on THE Best/compare/Extrinsic	1 2 3 4 5 6 7 8 9 10	Focus on MY Best/share/Intrinsic
Totally degraded others	1 2 3 4 5 6 7 8 9 10	Totally respected others
Totally belittled self	1 2 3 4 5 6 7 8 9 10	Totally respected self
Nada zip zero preparation/progress	1 2 3 4 5 6 7 8 9 10	Amazing preparation/progress
Total manipulation of others	1 2 3 4 5 6 7 8 9 10	No manipulation of others
Awful. Hated it. Grudges dragging	1 2 3 4 5 6 7 8 9 10	Great! Fun! No inner reservations. Flow/Zone

REFLECTIONS	Comments
Thoughts/feelings effecting output	
Possible cause of positive/negative changes	
Patterns or helpful observations	
Input from leader/mentor/friend	
Insights:	

Name _____ Cl _____

Core Power Pro-Launch Pad:
Propel Progress 12

Practice or performance (circle one)	**Date:**
TYPE of performance (circle) Tests/Sports/Business/Performing Arts/Other:	
Observed problem/s:	

Last goal completed? (circle)
Yes/No

Type of Goal: (circle) Performance Ability/Emotional IQ/Life Balance/Respect self/Respect Others/No manipulation/Take Responsibility/Other:

Goal/s:

Observations	Notes
What happens	
When	
Where	
Why	
How Much	

OBSERVATIONS	Circle	Practice Performance (circle)
Worst ever quality	1 2 3 4 5 6 7 8 9 10	Awesome over-all quality
Incapacitating anxiety, Totally unsure	1 2 3 4 5 6 7 8 9 10	Great flow/zone, Totally sure
Focus on THE Best/compare/Extrinsic	1 2 3 4 5 6 7 8 9 10	Focus on MY Best/share/Intrinsic
Totally degraded others	1 2 3 4 5 6 7 8 9 10	Totally respected others
Totally belittled self	1 2 3 4 5 6 7 8 9 10	Totally respected self
Nada zip zero preparation/progress	1 2 3 4 5 6 7 8 9 10	Amazing preparation/progress
Total manipulation of others	1 2 3 4 5 6 7 8 9 10	No manipulation of others
Awful. Hated it. Grudges dragging	1 2 3 4 5 6 7 8 9 10	Great! Fun! No inner reservations. Flow/Zone

REFLECTIONS	Comments
Thoughts/feelings effecting output	
Possible cause of positive/negative changes	
Patterns or helpful observations	
Input from leader/mentor/friend	
Insights:	

Name _____ Cl _____

Phase II.

Propel Progress
Application Phase

B

Increase Ability
Building core ability through directed observations
during practice and performance.

Notice thoughts and feelings.
Notice influences affecting ability.
Set realistic but challenging goals every time.
Always evaluate whether the goal was achieved.
Build sequentially on past goals and achievements.
If ability changes, *something* changed; find out why.

Core Power Pro-Launch Pad:
Propel Progress 1

Practice or performance (circle one)	**Date:**
TYPE of performance (circle) Tests/Sports/Business/Performing Arts/Other:	
Observed problem/s:	

Yes/No	**Last goal completed?** (circle)
Type of Goal: (circle) Performance Ability/Emotional IQ/Life Balance/Respect self/Respect Others/No manipulation/Take Responsibility/Other:	
Goal/s:	

Observations	Notes
What happens	
When	
Where	
Why	
How Much	

OBSERVATIONS	Circle	Practice Performance (circle)
Worst ever quality	1 2 3 4 5 6 7 8 9 10	Awesome over-all quality
Incapacitating anxiety, Totally unsure	1 2 3 4 5 6 7 8 9 10	Great flow/zone, Totally sure
Focus on THE Best/compare/Extrinsic	1 2 3 4 5 6 7 8 9 10	Focus on MY Best/share/Intrinsic
Totally degraded others	1 2 3 4 5 6 7 8 9 10	Totally respected others
Totally belittled self	1 2 3 4 5 6 7 8 9 10	Totally respected self
Nada zip zero preparation/progress	1 2 3 4 5 6 7 8 9 10	Amazing preparation/progress
Total manipulation of others	1 2 3 4 5 6 7 8 9 10	No manipulation of others
Awful. Hated it. Grudges dragging	1 2 3 4 5 6 7 8 9 10	Great! Fun! No inner reservations. Flow/Zone

REFLECTIONS	Comments
Thoughts/feelings effecting output	
Possible cause of positive/negative changes	
Patterns or helpful observations	
Input from leader/mentor/friend	

Insights:

Name _____ Cl _____

Core Power Pro-Launch Pad:
Propel Progress 2

Practice or performance (circle one)	**Date:**

TYPE of performance (circle) Tests/Sports/Business/Performing Arts/Other:

Observed problem/s:

Last goal completed? (circle) **Yes/No**

Type of Goal: (circle) Performance Ability/Emotional IQ/Life Balance/Respect self/Respect Others/No manipulation/Take Responsibility/Other:

Goal/s:

Observations	Notes
What happens	
When	
Where	
Why	
How Much	

OBSERVATIONS	Circle	Practice Performance (circle)
Worst ever quality	1 2 3 4 5 6 7 8 9 10	Awesome over-all quality
Incapacitating anxiety, Totally unsure	1 2 3 4 5 6 7 8 9 10	Great flow/zone, Totally sure
Focus on THE Best/compare/Extrinsic	1 2 3 4 5 6 7 8 9 10	Focus on MY Best/share/Intrinsic
Totally degraded others	1 2 3 4 5 6 7 8 9 10	Totally respected others
Totally belittled self	1 2 3 4 5 6 7 8 9 10	Totally respected self
Nada zip zero preparation/progress	1 2 3 4 5 6 7 8 9 10	Amazing preparation/progress
Total manipulation of others	1 2 3 4 5 6 7 8 9 10	No manipulation of others
Awful. Hated it. Grudges dragging	1 2 3 4 5 6 7 8 9 10	Great! Fun! No inner reservations. Flow/Zone

REFLECTIONS	Comments
Thoughts/feelings effecting output	
Possible cause of positive/negative changes	
Patterns or helpful observations	
Input from leader/mentor/friend	
Insights:	

Name _____ Cl _____

Core Power Pro-Launch Pad:
Propel Progress 3

Practice or performance (circle one)	**Date:**

TYPE of performance (circle) Tests/Sports/Business/Performing Arts/Other:

Observed problem/s:

Last goal completed? (circle)
Yes/No

Type of Goal: (circle) Performance Ability/Emotional IQ/Life Balance/Respect self/Respect Others/No manipulation/Take Responsibility/Other:

Goal/s:

Observations	Notes
What happens	
When	
Where	
Why	
How Much	

OBSERVATIONS	Circle	Practice Performance (circle)
Worst ever quality	1 2 3 4 5 6 7 8 9 10	Awesome over-all quality
Incapacitating anxiety, Totally unsure	1 2 3 4 5 6 7 8 9 10	Great flow/zone, Totally sure
Focus on THE Best/compare/Extrinsic	1 2 3 4 5 6 7 8 9 10	Focus on MY Best/share/Intrinsic
Totally degraded others	1 2 3 4 5 6 7 8 9 10	Totally respected others
Totally belittled self	1 2 3 4 5 6 7 8 9 10	Totally respected self
Nada zip zero preparation/progress	1 2 3 4 5 6 7 8 9 10	Amazing preparation/progress
Total manipulation of others	1 2 3 4 5 6 7 8 9 10	No manipulation of others
Awful. Hated it. Grudges dragging	1 2 3 4 5 6 7 8 9 10	Great! Fun! No inner reservations. Flow/Zone

REFLECTIONS	Comments
Thoughts/feelings effecting output	
Possible cause of positive/negative changes	
Patterns or helpful observations	
Input from leader/mentor/friend	
Insights:	

Name _____ Cl _____

Core Power Pro-Launch Pad:
Propel Progress 4

Practice or performance (circle one)   **Date:**

TYPE of performance (circle) Tests/Sports/Business/Performing Arts/Other:

Observed problem/s:

Last goal completed? (circle)
Yes/No

Type of Goal: (circle) Performance Ability/Emotional IQ/Life Balance/Respect self/Respect Others/No manipulation/Take Responsibility/Other:

Goal/s:

Observations	Notes
What happens	
When	
Where	
Why	
How Much	

OBSERVATIONS	Circle	Practice Performance (circle)
Worst ever quality	1 2 3 4 5 6 7 8 9 10	Awesome over-all quality
Incapacitating anxiety, Totally unsure	1 2 3 4 5 6 7 8 9 10	Great flow/zone, Totally sure
Focus on THE Best/compare/Extrinsic	1 2 3 4 5 6 7 8 9 10	Focus on MY Best/share/Intrinsic
Totally degraded others	1 2 3 4 5 6 7 8 9 10	Totally respected others
Totally belittled self	1 2 3 4 5 6 7 8 9 10	Totally respected self
Nada zip zero preparation/progress	1 2 3 4 5 6 7 8 9 10	Amazing preparation/progress
Total manipulation of others	1 2 3 4 5 6 7 8 9 10	No manipulation of others
Awful. Hated it. Grudges dragging	1 2 3 4 5 6 7 8 9 10	Great! Fun! No inner reservations. Flow/Zone

REFLECTIONS	Comments
Thoughts/feelings effecting output	
Possible cause of positive/negative changes	
Patterns or helpful observations	
Input from leader/mentor/friend	
Insights:	

Name _____ Cl _____

Core Power Pro-Launch Pad:
Propel Progress 5

Practice or performance (circle one)   **Date:**

TYPE of performance (circle) Tests/Sports/Business/Performing Arts/Other:

Observed problem/s:

Last goal completed? (circle)
Yes/No

Type of Goal: (circle) Performance Ability/Emotional IQ/Life Balance/Respect self/Respect Others/No manipulation/Take Responsibility/Other:

Goal/s:

Observations	Notes
What happens	
When	
Where	
Why	
How Much	

OBSERVATIONS	Circle	Practice Performance (circle)
Worst ever quality	1 2 3 4 5 6 7 8 9 10	Awesome over-all quality
Incapacitating anxiety, Totally unsure	1 2 3 4 5 6 7 8 9 10	Great flow/zone, Totally sure
Focus on THE Best/compare/Extrinsic	1 2 3 4 5 6 7 8 9 10	Focus on MY Best/share/Intrinsic
Totally degraded others	1 2 3 4 5 6 7 8 9 10	Totally respected others
Totally belittled self	1 2 3 4 5 6 7 8 9 10	Totally respected self
Nada zip zero preparation/progress	1 2 3 4 5 6 7 8 9 10	Amazing preparation/progress
Total manipulation of others	1 2 3 4 5 6 7 8 9 10	No manipulation of others
Awful. Hated it. Grudges dragging	1 2 3 4 5 6 7 8 9 10	Great! Fun! No inner reservations. Flow/Zone

REFLECTIONS	Comments
Thoughts/feelings effecting output	
Possible cause of positive/negative changes	
Patterns or helpful observations	
Input from leader/mentor/friend	
Insights:	

Name _____ Cl _____

Core Power Pro-Launch Pad:
Propel Progress 6

Practice or performance (circle one)	**Date:**

TYPE of performance (circle) Tests/Sports/Business/Performing Arts/Other:

Observed problem/s:

Last goal completed? (circle)
Yes/No

Type of Goal: (circle) Performance Ability/Emotional IQ/Life Balance/Respect self/Respect Others/No manipulation/Take Responsibility/Other:

Goal/s:

Observations	Notes
What happens	
When	
Where	
Why	
How Much	

OBSERVATIONS	Circle	Practice Performance (circle)
Worst ever quality	1 2 3 4 5 6 7 8 9 10	Awesome over-all quality
Incapacitating anxiety, Totally unsure	1 2 3 4 5 6 7 8 9 10	Great flow/zone, Totally sure
Focus on THE Best/compare/Extrinsic	1 2 3 4 5 6 7 8 9 10	Focus on MY Best/share/Intrinsic
Totally degraded others	1 2 3 4 5 6 7 8 9 10	Totally respected others
Totally belittled self	1 2 3 4 5 6 7 8 9 10	Totally respected self
Nada zip zero preparation/progress	1 2 3 4 5 6 7 8 9 10	Amazing preparation/progress
Total manipulation of others	1 2 3 4 5 6 7 8 9 10	No manipulation of others
Awful. Hated it. Grudges dragging	1 2 3 4 5 6 7 8 9 10	Great! Fun! No inner reservations. Flow/Zone

REFLECTIONS	Comments
Thoughts/feelings effecting output	
Possible cause of positive/negative changes	
Patterns or helpful observations	
Input from leader/mentor/friend	
Insights:	

Name _____ Cl _____

Core Power Pro-Launch Pad:
Propel Progress 7

Practice or performance (circle one)	**Date:**

TYPE of performance (circle) Tests/Sports/Business/Performing Arts/Other:

Observed problem/s:

Yes/No	**Last goal completed?** (circle)

Type of Goal: (circle) Performance Ability/Emotional IQ/Life Balance/Respect self/Respect Others/No manipulation/Take Responsibility/Other:

Goal/s:

Observations	Notes
What happens	
When	
Where	
Why	
How Much	

OBSERVATIONS	Circle	Practice Performance (circle)
Worst ever quality	1 2 3 4 5 6 7 8 9 10	Awesome over-all quality
Incapacitating anxiety, Totally unsure	1 2 3 4 5 6 7 8 9 10	Great flow/zone, Totally sure
Focus on THE Best/compare/Extrinsic	1 2 3 4 5 6 7 8 9 10	Focus on MY Best/share/Intrinsic
Totally degraded others	1 2 3 4 5 6 7 8 9 10	Totally respected others
Totally belittled self	1 2 3 4 5 6 7 8 9 10	Totally respected self
Nada zip zero preparation/progress	1 2 3 4 5 6 7 8 9 10	Amazing preparation/progress
Total manipulation of others	1 2 3 4 5 6 7 8 9 10	No manipulation of others
Awful. Hated it. Grudges dragging	1 2 3 4 5 6 7 8 9 10	Great! Fun! No inner reservations. Flow/Zone

REFLECTIONS	Comments
Thoughts/feelings effecting output	
Possible cause of positive/negative changes	
Patterns or helpful observations	
Input from leader/mentor/friend	
Insights:	

Name _____ Cl _____

Core Power Pro-Launch Pad:
Propel Progress 8

Practice or performance (circle one)   **Date:**

TYPE of performance (circle) Tests/Sports/Business/Performing Arts/Other:

Observed problem/s:

Last goal completed? (circle)
Yes/No

Type of Goal: (circle) Performance Ability/Emotional IQ/Life Balance/Respect self/Respect Others/No manipulation/Take Responsibility/Other:

Goal/s:

Observations	Notes
What happens	
When	
Where	
Why	
How Much	

OBSERVATIONS	Circle	Practice Performance (circle)
Worst ever quality	1 2 3 4 5 6 7 8 9 10	Awesome over-all quality
Incapacitating anxiety, Totally unsure	1 2 3 4 5 6 7 8 9 10	Great flow/zone, Totally sure
Focus on THE Best/compare/Extrinsic	1 2 3 4 5 6 7 8 9 10	Focus on MY Best/share/Intrinsic
Totally degraded others	1 2 3 4 5 6 7 8 9 10	Totally respected others
Totally belittled self	1 2 3 4 5 6 7 8 9 10	Totally respected self
Nada zip zero preparation/progress	1 2 3 4 5 6 7 8 9 10	Amazing preparation/progress
Total manipulation of others	1 2 3 4 5 6 7 8 9 10	No manipulation of others
Awful. Hated it. Grudges dragging	1 2 3 4 5 6 7 8 9 10	Great! Fun! No inner reservations. Flow/Zone

REFLECTIONS	Comments
Thoughts/feelings effecting output	
Possible cause of positive/negative changes	
Patterns or helpful observations	
Input from leader/mentor/friend	
Insights:	

Name _____ Cl _____

Core Power Pro-Launch Pad:
Propel Progress 9

Practice or performance (circle one)	**Date:**

TYPE of performance (circle) Tests/Sports/Business/Performing Arts/Other:

Observed problem/s:

Last goal completed? (circle)	
Yes/No	

Type of Goal: (circle) Performance Ability/Emotional IQ/Life Balance/Respect self/Respect Others/No manipulation/Take Responsibility/Other:

Goal/s:

Observations	Notes
What happens	
When	
Where	
Why	
How Much	

OBSERVATIONS	Circle	Practice Performance (circle)
Worst ever quality	1 2 3 4 5 6 7 8 9 10	Awesome over-all quality
Incapacitating anxiety, Totally unsure	1 2 3 4 5 6 7 8 9 10	Great flow/zone, Totally sure
Focus on THE Best/compare/Extrinsic	1 2 3 4 5 6 7 8 9 10	Focus on MY Best/share/Intrinsic
Totally degraded others	1 2 3 4 5 6 7 8 9 10	Totally respected others
Totally belittled self	1 2 3 4 5 6 7 8 9 10	Totally respected self
Nada zip zero preparation/progress	1 2 3 4 5 6 7 8 9 10	Amazing preparation/progress
Total manipulation of others	1 2 3 4 5 6 7 8 9 10	No manipulation of others
Awful. Hated it. Grudges dragging	1 2 3 4 5 6 7 8 9 10	Great! Fun! No inner reservations. Flow/Zone

REFLECTIONS	Comments
Thoughts/feelings effecting output	
Possible cause of positive/negative changes	
Patterns or helpful observations	
Input from leader/mentor/friend	
Insights:	

Name _____ Cl _____

Core Power Pro-Launch Pad:
Propel Progress 10

Practice or performance (circle one)	**Date:**

TYPE of performance (circle) Tests/Sports/Business/Performing Arts/Other:

Observed problem/s:

Last goal completed? (circle)
Yes/No

Type of Goal: (circle) Performance Ability/Emotional IQ/Life Balance/Respect self/Respect Others/No manipulation/Take Responsibility/Other:

Goal/s:

Observations	Notes
What happens	
When	
Where	
Why	
How Much	

OBSERVATIONS	Circle	Practice Performance (circle)
Worst ever quality	1 2 3 4 5 6 7 8 9 10	Awesome over-all quality
Incapacitating anxiety, Totally unsure	1 2 3 4 5 6 7 8 9 10	Great flow/zone, Totally sure
Focus on THE Best/compare/Extrinsic	1 2 3 4 5 6 7 8 9 10	Focus on MY Best/share/Intrinsic
Totally degraded others	1 2 3 4 5 6 7 8 9 10	Totally respected others
Totally belittled self	1 2 3 4 5 6 7 8 9 10	Totally respected self
Nada zip zero preparation/progress	1 2 3 4 5 6 7 8 9 10	Amazing preparation/progress
Total manipulation of others	1 2 3 4 5 6 7 8 9 10	No manipulation of others
Awful. Hated it. Grudges dragging	1 2 3 4 5 6 7 8 9 10	Great! Fun! No inner reservations. Flow/Zone

REFLECTIONS	Comments
Thoughts/feelings effecting output	
Possible cause of positive/negative changes	
Patterns or helpful observations	
Input from leader/mentor/friend	
Insights:	

Name _____ Cl _____

Core Power Pro-Launch Pad:
Propel Progress 11

Practice or performance (circle one)　　　　　**Date:**

TYPE of performance (circle) Tests/Sports/Business/Performing Arts/Other:

Observed problem/s:

Last goal completed? (circle)
Yes/No

Type of Goal: (circle) Performance Ability/Emotional IQ/Life Balance/Respect self/Respect Others/No manipulation/Take Responsibility/Other:

Goal/s:

Observations	Notes
What happens	
When	
Where	
Why	
How Much	

OBSERVATIONS	Circle	Practice Performance (circle)
Worst ever quality	1 2 3 4 5 6 7 8 9 10	Awesome over-all quality
Incapacitating anxiety, Totally unsure	1 2 3 4 5 6 7 8 9 10	Great flow/zone, Totally sure
Focus on THE Best/compare/Extrinsic	1 2 3 4 5 6 7 8 9 10	Focus on MY Best/share/Intrinsic
Totally degraded others	1 2 3 4 5 6 7 8 9 10	Totally respected others
Totally belittled self	1 2 3 4 5 6 7 8 9 10	Totally respected self
Nada zip zero preparation/progress	1 2 3 4 5 6 7 8 9 10	Amazing preparation/progress
Total manipulation of others	1 2 3 4 5 6 7 8 9 10	No manipulation of others
Awful. Hated it. Grudges dragging	1 2 3 4 5 6 7 8 9 10	Great! Fun! No inner reservations. Flow/Zone

REFLECTIONS	Comments
Thoughts/feelings effecting output	
Possible cause of positive/negative changes	
Patterns or helpful observations	
Input from leader/mentor/friend	
Insights:	

Name _____ Cl _____

Core Power Pro-Launch Pad:
Propel Progress 12

Practice or performance (circle one)   **Date:**

TYPE of performance (circle) Tests/Sports/Business/Performing Arts/Other:

Observed problem/s:

Last goal completed? (circle)
Yes/No

Type of Goal: (circle) Performance Ability/Emotional IQ/Life Balance/Respect self/Respect Others/No manipulation/Take Responsibility/Other:

Goal/s:

Observations	Notes
What happens	
When	
Where	
Why	
How Much	

OBSERVATIONS	Circle	Practice Performance (circle)
Worst ever quality	1 2 3 4 5 6 7 8 9 10	Awesome over-all quality
Incapacitating anxiety, Totally unsure	1 2 3 4 5 6 7 8 9 10	Great flow/zone, Totally sure
Focus on THE Best/compare/Extrinsic	1 2 3 4 5 6 7 8 9 10	Focus on MY Best/share/Intrinsic
Totally degraded others	1 2 3 4 5 6 7 8 9 10	Totally respected others
Totally belittled self	1 2 3 4 5 6 7 8 9 10	Totally respected self
Nada zip zero preparation/progress	1 2 3 4 5 6 7 8 9 10	Amazing preparation/progress
Total manipulation of others	1 2 3 4 5 6 7 8 9 10	No manipulation of others
Awful. Hated it. Grudges dragging	1 2 3 4 5 6 7 8 9 10	Great! Fun! No inner reservations. Flow/Zone

REFLECTIONS	Comments
Thoughts/feelings effecting output	
Possible cause of positive/negative changes	
Patterns or helpful observations	
Input from leader/mentor/friend	
Insights:	

Name _____ Cl _____

Phase III.

Propel Progress
Application Phase

C

Increase Ability
Building core ability through directed observations
during practice and performance.

Notice thoughts and feelings.
Notice influences affecting ability.
Set realistic but challenging goals every time.
Always evaluate whether the goal was achieved.
Build sequentially on past goals and achievements.
If ability changes, *something* changed; find out why.

Core Power Pro-Launch Pad:
Propel Progress 1

Practice or performance (circle one)	**Date:**

TYPE of performance (circle) Tests/Sports/Business/Performing Arts/Other:

Observed problem/s:

Yes/No	**Last goal completed?** (circle)

Type of Goal: (circle) Performance Ability/Emotional IQ/Life Balance/Respect self/Respect Others/No manipulation/Take Responsibility/Other:

Goal/s:

Observations	Notes
What happens	
When	
Where	
Why	
How Much	

OBSERVATIONS	Circle	Practice Performance (circle)
Worst ever quality	1 2 3 4 5 6 7 8 9 10	Awesome over-all quality
Incapacitating anxiety, Totally unsure	1 2 3 4 5 6 7 8 9 10	Great flow/zone, Totally sure
Focus on THE Best/compare/Extrinsic	1 2 3 4 5 6 7 8 9 10	Focus on MY Best/share/Intrinsic
Totally degraded others	1 2 3 4 5 6 7 8 9 10	Totally respected others
Totally belittled self	1 2 3 4 5 6 7 8 9 10	Totally respected self
Nada zip zero preparation/progress	1 2 3 4 5 6 7 8 9 10	Amazing preparation/progress
Total manipulation of others	1 2 3 4 5 6 7 8 9 10	No manipulation of others
Awful. Hated it. Grudges dragging	1 2 3 4 5 6 7 8 9 10	Great! Fun! No inner reservations. Flow/Zone

REFLECTIONS	Comments
Thoughts/feelings effecting output	
Possible cause of positive/negative changes	
Patterns or helpful observations	
Input from leader/mentor/friend	
Insights:	

Name _____ Cl _____

Core Power Pro-Launch Pad:
Propel Progress 2

Practice or performance (circle one)   **Date:**

TYPE of performance (circle) Tests/Sports/Business/Performing Arts/Other:

Observed problem/s:

Last goal completed? (circle)
Yes/No

Type of Goal: (circle) Performance Ability/Emotional IQ/Life Balance/Respect self/Respect Others/No manipulation/Take Responsibility/Other:

Goal/s:

Observations	Notes
What happens	
When	
Where	
Why	
How Much	

OBSERVATIONS	Circle	Practice Performance (circle)
Worst ever quality	1 2 3 4 5 6 7 8 9 10	Awesome over-all quality
Incapacitating anxiety, Totally unsure	1 2 3 4 5 6 7 8 9 10	Great flow/zone, Totally sure
Focus on THE Best/compare/Extrinsic	1 2 3 4 5 6 7 8 9 10	Focus on MY Best/share/Intrinsic
Totally degraded others	1 2 3 4 5 6 7 8 9 10	Totally respected others
Totally belittled self	1 2 3 4 5 6 7 8 9 10	Totally respected self
Nada zip zero preparation/progress	1 2 3 4 5 6 7 8 9 10	Amazing preparation/progress
Total manipulation of others	1 2 3 4 5 6 7 8 9 10	No manipulation of others
Awful. Hated it. Grudges dragging	1 2 3 4 5 6 7 8 9 10	Great! Fun! No inner reservations. Flow/Zone

REFLECTIONS	Comments
Thoughts/feelings effecting output	
Possible cause of positive/negative changes	
Patterns or helpful observations	
Input from leader/mentor/friend	
Insights:	

Name _____ Cl _____

Core Power Pro-Launch Pad:
Propel Progress 3

Practice or performance (circle one)   **Date:**

TYPE of performance (circle) Tests/Sports/Business/Performing Arts/Other:

Observed problem/s:

Last goal completed? (circle)

Yes/No

Type of Goal: (circle) Performance Ability/Emotional IQ/Life Balance/Respect self/Respect Others/No manipulation/Take Responsibility/Other:

Goal/s:

Observations	Notes
What happens	
When	
Where	
Why	
How Much	

OBSERVATIONS	Circle	Practice Performance (circle)
Worst ever quality	1 2 3 4 5 6 7 8 9 10	Awesome over-all quality
Incapacitating anxiety, Totally unsure	1 2 3 4 5 6 7 8 9 10	Great flow/zone, Totally sure
Focus on THE Best/compare/Extrinsic	1 2 3 4 5 6 7 8 9 10	Focus on MY Best/share/Intrinsic
Totally degraded others	1 2 3 4 5 6 7 8 9 10	Totally respected others
Totally belittled self	1 2 3 4 5 6 7 8 9 10	Totally respected self
Nada zip zero preparation/progress	1 2 3 4 5 6 7 8 9 10	Amazing preparation/progress
Total manipulation of others	1 2 3 4 5 6 7 8 9 10	No manipulation of others
Awful. Hated it. Grudges dragging	1 2 3 4 5 6 7 8 9 10	Great! Fun! No inner reservations. Flow/Zone

REFLECTIONS	Comments
Thoughts/feelings effecting output	
Possible cause of positive/negative changes	
Patterns or helpful observations	
Input from leader/mentor/friend	
Insights:	

Name _____ Cl _____

Core Power Pro-Launch Pad:
Propel Progress 4

Practice or performance (circle one)	**Date:**
TYPE of performance (circle) Tests/Sports/Business/Performing Arts/Other:	
Observed problem/s:	

Last goal completed? (circle) **Yes/No**
Type of Goal: (circle) Performance Ability/Emotional IQ/Life Balance/Respect self/Respect Others/No manipulation/Take Responsibility/Other:
Goal/s:

Observations	Notes
What happens	
When	
Where	
Why	
How Much	

OBSERVATIONS	Circle	Practice Performance (circle)
Worst ever quality	1 2 3 4 5 6 7 8 9 10	Awesome over-all quality
Incapacitating anxiety, Totally unsure	1 2 3 4 5 6 7 8 9 10	Great flow/zone, Totally sure
Focus on THE Best/compare/Extrinsic	1 2 3 4 5 6 7 8 9 10	Focus on MY Best/share/Intrinsic
Totally degraded others	1 2 3 4 5 6 7 8 9 10	Totally respected others
Totally belittled self	1 2 3 4 5 6 7 8 9 10	Totally respected self
Nada zip zero preparation/progress	1 2 3 4 5 6 7 8 9 10	Amazing preparation/progress
Total manipulation of others	1 2 3 4 5 6 7 8 9 10	No manipulation of others
Awful. Hated it. Grudges dragging	1 2 3 4 5 6 7 8 9 10	Great! Fun! No inner reservations. Flow/Zone

REFLECTIONS	Comments
Thoughts/feelings effecting output	
Possible cause of positive/negative changes	
Patterns or helpful observations	
Input from leader/mentor/friend	

Insights:

Name _____ Cl _____

Core Power Pro-Launch Pad:
Propel Progress 5

Practice or performance (circle one)   **Date:**

TYPE of performance (circle) Tests/Sports/Business/Performing Arts/Other:

Observed problem/s:

Last goal completed? (circle)
Yes/No

Type of Goal: (circle) Performance Ability/Emotional IQ/Life Balance/Respect
self/Respect Others/No manipulation/Take Responsibility/Other:

Goal/s:

Observations	Notes
What happens	
When	
Where	
Why	
How Much	

OBSERVATIONS	Circle	Practice Performance (circle)
Worst ever quality	1 2 3 4 5 6 7 8 9 10	Awesome over-all quality
Incapacitating anxiety, Totally unsure	1 2 3 4 5 6 7 8 9 10	Great flow/zone, Totally sure
Focus on THE Best/compare/Extrinsic	1 2 3 4 5 6 7 8 9 10	Focus on MY Best/share/Intrinsic
Totally degraded others	1 2 3 4 5 6 7 8 9 10	Totally respected others
Totally belittled self	1 2 3 4 5 6 7 8 9 10	Totally respected self
Nada zip zero preparation/progress	1 2 3 4 5 6 7 8 9 10	Amazing preparation/progress
Total manipulation of others	1 2 3 4 5 6 7 8 9 10	No manipulation of others
Awful. Hated it. Grudges dragging	1 2 3 4 5 6 7 8 9 10	Great! Fun! No inner reservations. Flow/Zone

REFLECTIONS	Comments
Thoughts/feelings effecting output	
Possible cause of positive/negative changes	
Patterns or helpful observations	
Input from leader/mentor/friend	
Insights:	

Name _____ Cl _____

Core Power Pro-Launch Pad:
Propel Progress 6

Practice or performance (circle one)	**Date:**
TYPE of performance (circle) Tests/Sports/Business/Performing Arts/Other:	
Observed problem/s:	

Last goal completed? (circle) **Yes/No**	
Type of Goal: (circle) Performance Ability/Emotional IQ/Life Balance/Respect self/Respect Others/No manipulation/Take Responsibility/Other:	
Goal/s:	

Observations	Notes
What happens	
When	
Where	
Why	
How Much	

183

Ta

CORE POWER PRO-LAUNCH PAD

OBSERVATIONS	Circle	Practice Performance (circle)
Worst ever quality	1 2 3 4 5 6 7 8 9 10	Awesome over-all quality
Incapacitating anxiety, Totally unsure	1 2 3 4 5 6 7 8 9 10	Great flow/zone, Totally sure
Focus on THE Best/compare/Extrinsic	1 2 3 4 5 6 7 8 9 10	Focus on MY Best/share/Intrinsic
Totally degraded others	1 2 3 4 5 6 7 8 9 10	Totally respected others
Totally belittled self	1 2 3 4 5 6 7 8 9 10	Totally respected self
Nada zip zero preparation/progress	1 2 3 4 5 6 7 8 9 10	Amazing preparation/progress
Total manipulation of others	1 2 3 4 5 6 7 8 9 10	No manipulation of others
Awful. Hated it. Grudges dragging	1 2 3 4 5 6 7 8 9 10	Great! Fun! No inner reservations. Flow/Zone

REFLECTIONS	Comments
Thoughts/feelings effecting output	
Possible cause of positive/negative changes	
Patterns or helpful observations	
Input from leader/mentor/friend	
Insights:	

©2018 All rights reserved

Name _____ Cl _____

184

Core Power Pro-Launch Pad:
Propel Progress 7

Practice or performance (circle one)	**Date:**
TYPE of performance (circle) Tests/Sports/Business/Performing Arts/Other:	
Observed problem/s:	

Last goal completed? (circle)   Yes/No
Type of Goal: (circle) Performance Ability/Emotional IQ/Life Balance/Respect self/Respect Others/No manipulation/Take Responsibility/Other:
Goal/s:

Observations	Notes
What happens	
When	
Where	
Why	
How Much	

OBSERVATIONS	Circle	Practice Performance (circle)
Worst ever quality	1 2 3 4 5 6 7 8 9 10	Awesome over-all quality
Incapacitating anxiety, Totally unsure	1 2 3 4 5 6 7 8 9 10	Great flow/zone, Totally sure
Focus on THE Best/compare/Extrinsic	1 2 3 4 5 6 7 8 9 10	Focus on MY Best/share/Intrinsic
Totally degraded others	1 2 3 4 5 6 7 8 9 10	Totally respected others
Totally belittled self	1 2 3 4 5 6 7 8 9 10	Totally respected self
Nada zip zero preparation/progress	1 2 3 4 5 6 7 8 9 10	Amazing preparation/progress
Total manipulation of others	1 2 3 4 5 6 7 8 9 10	No manipulation of others
Awful. Hated it. Grudges dragging	1 2 3 4 5 6 7 8 9 10	Great! Fun! No inner reservations. Flow/Zone

REFLECTIONS	Comments
Thoughts/feelings effecting output	
Possible cause of positive/negative changes	
Patterns or helpful observations	
Input from leader/mentor/friend	
Insights:	

Name _____ Cl _____

Core Power Pro-Launch Pad:
Propel Progress 8

Practice or performance (circle one)	**Date:**
TYPE of performance (circle) Tests/Sports/Business/Performing Arts/Other:	
Observed problem/s:	

Last goal completed? (circle) **Yes/No**	
Type of Goal: (circle) Performance Ability/Emotional IQ/Life Balance/Respect self/Respect Others/No manipulation/Take Responsibility/Other:	
Goal/s:	

Observations	Notes
What happens	
When	
Where	
Why	
How Much	

OBSERVATIONS	Circle	Practice Performance (circle)
Worst ever quality	1 2 3 4 5 6 7 8 9 10	Awesome over-all quality
Incapacitating anxiety, Totally unsure	1 2 3 4 5 6 7 8 9 10	Great flow/zone, Totally sure
Focus on THE Best/compare/Extrinsic	1 2 3 4 5 6 7 8 9 10	Focus on MY Best/share/Intrinsic
Totally degraded others	1 2 3 4 5 6 7 8 9 10	Totally respected others
Totally belittled self	1 2 3 4 5 6 7 8 9 10	Totally respected self
Nada zip zero preparation/progress	1 2 3 4 5 6 7 8 9 10	Amazing preparation/progress
Total manipulation of others	1 2 3 4 5 6 7 8 9 10	No manipulation of others
Awful. Hated it. Grudges dragging	1 2 3 4 5 6 7 8 9 10	Great! Fun! No inner reservations. Flow/Zone

REFLECTIONS	Comments
Thoughts/feelings effecting output	
Possible cause of positive/negative changes	
Patterns or helpful observations	
Input from leader/mentor/friend	
Insights:	

Name _____ Cl _____

Core Power Pro-Launch Pad:
Propel Progress 9

Practice or performance (circle one)	**Date:**

TYPE of performance (circle) Tests/Sports/Business/Performing Arts/Other:

Observed problem/s:

Last goal completed? (circle)
Yes/No

Type of Goal: (circle) Performance Ability/Emotional IQ/Life Balance/Respect self/Respect Others/No manipulation/Take Responsibility/Other:

Goal/s:

Observations	Notes
What happens	
When	
Where	
Why	
How Much	

OBSERVATIONS	Circle	Practice Performance (circle)
Worst ever quality	1 2 3 4 5 6 7 8 9 10	Awesome over-all quality
Incapacitating anxiety, Totally unsure	1 2 3 4 5 6 7 8 9 10	Great flow/zone, Totally sure
Focus on THE Best/compare/Extrinsic	1 2 3 4 5 6 7 8 9 10	Focus on MY Best/share/Intrinsic
Totally degraded others	1 2 3 4 5 6 7 8 9 10	Totally respected others
Totally belittled self	1 2 3 4 5 6 7 8 9 10	Totally respected self
Nada zip zero preparation/progress	1 2 3 4 5 6 7 8 9 10	Amazing preparation/progress
Total manipulation of others	1 2 3 4 5 6 7 8 9 10	No manipulation of others
Awful. Hated it. Grudges dragging	1 2 3 4 5 6 7 8 9 10	Great! Fun! No inner reservations. Flow/Zone

REFLECTIONS	Comments
Thoughts/feelings effecting output	
Possible cause of positive/negative changes	
Patterns or helpful observations	
Input from leader/mentor/friend	
Insights:	

Name _____ Cl _____

Core Power Pro-Launch Pad:
Propel Progress 10

Practice or performance (circle one)	**Date:**

TYPE of performance (circle) Tests/Sports/Business/Performing Arts/Other:

Observed problem/s:

Last goal completed? (circle)
Yes/No

Type of Goal: (circle) Performance Ability/Emotional IQ/Life Balance/Respect self/Respect Others/No manipulation/Take Responsibility/Other:

Goal/s:

Observations	Notes
What happens	
When	
Where	
Why	
How Much	

OBSERVATIONS	Circle	Practice Performance (circle)
Worst ever quality	1 2 3 4 5 6 7 8 9 10	Awesome over-all quality
Incapacitating anxiety, Totally unsure	1 2 3 4 5 6 7 8 9 10	Great flow/zone, Totally sure
Focus on THE Best/compare/Extrinsic	1 2 3 4 5 6 7 8 9 10	Focus on MY Best/share/Intrinsic
Totally degraded others	1 2 3 4 5 6 7 8 9 10	Totally respected others
Totally belittled self	1 2 3 4 5 6 7 8 9 10	Totally respected self
Nada zip zero preparation/progress	1 2 3 4 5 6 7 8 9 10	Amazing preparation/progress
Total manipulation of others	1 2 3 4 5 6 7 8 9 10	No manipulation of others
Awful. Hated it. Grudges dragging	1 2 3 4 5 6 7 8 9 10	Great! Fun! No inner reservations. Flow/Zone

REFLECTIONS	Comments
Thoughts/feelings effecting output	
Possible cause of positive/negative changes	
Patterns or helpful observations	
Input from leader/mentor/friend	

Insights:

Name _____ Cl _____

Core Power Pro-Launch Pad:
Propel Progress 11

Practice or performance (circle one)   **Date:**

TYPE of performance (circle) Tests/Sports/Business/Performing Arts/Other:

Observed problem/s:

Last goal completed? (circle)
Yes/No

Type of Goal: (circle) Performance Ability/Emotional IQ/Life Balance/Respect self/Respect Others/No manipulation/Take Responsibility/Other:

Goal/s:

Observations	Notes
What happens	
When	
Where	
Why	
How Much	

OBSERVATIONS	Circle	Practice Performance (circle)
Worst ever quality	1 2 3 4 5 6 7 8 9 10	Awesome over-all quality
Incapacitating anxiety, Totally unsure	1 2 3 4 5 6 7 8 9 10	Great flow/zone, Totally sure
Focus on THE Best/compare/Extrinsic	1 2 3 4 5 6 7 8 9 10	Focus on MY Best/share/Intrinsic
Totally degraded others	1 2 3 4 5 6 7 8 9 10	Totally respected others
Totally belittled self	1 2 3 4 5 6 7 8 9 10	Totally respected self
Nada zip zero preparation/progress	1 2 3 4 5 6 7 8 9 10	Amazing preparation/progress
Total manipulation of others	1 2 3 4 5 6 7 8 9 10	No manipulation of others
Awful. Hated it. Grudges dragging	1 2 3 4 5 6 7 8 9 10	Great! Fun! No inner reservations. Flow/Zone

REFLECTIONS	Comments
Thoughts/feelings effecting output	
Possible cause of positive/negative changes	
Patterns or helpful observations	
Input from leader/mentor/friend	
Insights:	

Name _____ Cl _____

Core Power Pro-Launch Pad:
Propel Progress 12

Practice or performance (circle one)	**Date:**
TYPE of performance (circle) Tests/Sports/Business/Performing Arts/Other:	
Observed problem/s:	

Last goal completed? (circle) **Yes/No**	
Type of Goal: (circle) Performance Ability/Emotional IQ/Life Balance/Respect self/Respect Others/No manipulation/Take Responsibility/Other:	
Goal/s:	

Observations	Notes
What happens	
When	
Where	
Why	
How Much	

OBSERVATIONS	Circle	Practice Performance (circle)
Worst ever quality	1 2 3 4 5 6 7 8 9 10	Awesome over-all quality
Incapacitating anxiety, Totally unsure	1 2 3 4 5 6 7 8 9 10	Great flow/zone, Totally sure
Focus on THE Best/compare/Extrinsic	1 2 3 4 5 6 7 8 9 10	Focus on MY Best/share/Intrinsic
Totally degraded others	1 2 3 4 5 6 7 8 9 10	Totally respected others
Totally belittled self	1 2 3 4 5 6 7 8 9 10	Totally respected self
Nada zip zero preparation/progress	1 2 3 4 5 6 7 8 9 10	Amazing preparation/progress
Total manipulation of others	1 2 3 4 5 6 7 8 9 10	No manipulation of others
Awful. Hated it. Grudges dragging	1 2 3 4 5 6 7 8 9 10	Great! Fun! No inner reservations. Flow/Zone

REFLECTIONS	Comments
Thoughts/feelings effecting output	
Possible cause of positive/negative changes	
Patterns or helpful observations	
Input from leader/mentor/friend	
Insights:	

Name _____ Cl _____

Phase IV.

Propel Progress

Application Phase

D

Increase Ability
Building core ability through directed observations
during practice and performance.

Notice thoughts and feelings.
Notice influences affecting ability.
Set realistic but challenging goals every time.
Always evaluate whether the goal was achieved.
Build sequentially on past goals and achievements.
If ability changes, *something* changed; find out why.

Core Power Pro-Launch Pad:
Propel Progress 1

Practice or performance (circle one)   **Date:**

TYPE of performance (circle) Tests/Sports/Business/Performing Arts/Other:

Observed problem/s:

Last goal completed? (circle) **Yes/No**

Type of Goal: (circle) Performance Ability/Emotional IQ/Life Balance/Respect self/Respect Others/No manipulation/Take Responsibility/Other:

Goal/s:

Observations	Notes
What happens	
When	
Where	
Why	
How Much	

OBSERVATIONS	Circle	Practice Performance (circle)
Worst ever quality	1 2 3 4 5 6 7 8 9 10	Awesome over-all quality
Incapacitating anxiety, Totally unsure	1 2 3 4 5 6 7 8 9 10	Great flow/zone, Totally sure
Focus on THE Best/compare/Extrinsic	1 2 3 4 5 6 7 8 9 10	Focus on MY Best/share/Intrinsic
Totally degraded others	1 2 3 4 5 6 7 8 9 10	Totally respected others
Totally belittled self	1 2 3 4 5 6 7 8 9 10	Totally respected self
Nada zip zero preparation/progress	1 2 3 4 5 6 7 8 9 10	Amazing preparation/progress
Total manipulation of others	1 2 3 4 5 6 7 8 9 10	No manipulation of others
Awful. Hated it. Grudges dragging	1 2 3 4 5 6 7 8 9 10	Great! Fun! No inner reservations. Flow/Zone

REFLECTIONS	Comments
Thoughts/feelings effecting output	
Possible cause of positive/negative changes	
Patterns or helpful observations	
Input from leader/mentor/friend	
Insights:	

Name _____ Cl _____

Core Power Pro-Launch Pad:
Propel Progress 2

Practice or performance (circle one)   **Date:**

TYPE of performance (circle) Tests/Sports/Business/Performing Arts/Other:

Observed problem/s:

Last goal completed? (circle) **Yes/No**

Type of Goal: (circle) Performance Ability/Emotional IQ/Life Balance/Respect self/Respect Others/No manipulation/Take Responsibility/Other:

Goal/s:

Observations	Notes
What happens	
When	
Where	
Why	
How Much	

OBSERVATIONS	Circle	Practice Performance (circle)
Worst ever quality	1 2 3 4 5 6 7 8 9 10	Awesome over-all quality
Incapacitating anxiety, Totally unsure	1 2 3 4 5 6 7 8 9 10	Great flow/zone, Totally sure
Focus on THE Best/compare/Extrinsic	1 2 3 4 5 6 7 8 9 10	Focus on MY Best/share/Intrinsic
Totally degraded others	1 2 3 4 5 6 7 8 9 10	Totally respected others
Totally belittled self	1 2 3 4 5 6 7 8 9 10	Totally respected self
Nada zip zero preparation/progress	1 2 3 4 5 6 7 8 9 10	Amazing preparation/progress
Total manipulation of others	1 2 3 4 5 6 7 8 9 10	No manipulation of others
Awful. Hated it. Grudges dragging	1 2 3 4 5 6 7 8 9 10	Great! Fun! No inner reservations. Flow/Zone

REFLECTIONS	Comments
Thoughts/feelings effecting output	
Possible cause of positive/negative changes	
Patterns or helpful observations	
Input from leader/mentor/friend	
Insights:	

Name _____ Cl _____

Core Power Pro-Launch Pad:
Propel Progress 3

Practice or performance (circle one)   **Date:**

TYPE of performance (circle) Tests/Sports/Business/Performing Arts/Other:

Observed problem/s:

Last goal completed? (circle) **Yes/No**

Type of Goal: (circle) Performance Ability/Emotional IQ/Life Balance/Respect self/Respect Others/No manipulation/Take Responsibility/Other:

Goal/s:

Observations	Notes
What happens	
When	
Where	
Why	
How Much	

OBSERVATIONS	Circle	Practice Performance (circle)
Worst ever quality	1 2 3 4 5 6 7 8 9 10	Awesome over-all quality
Incapacitating anxiety, Totally unsure	1 2 3 4 5 6 7 8 9 10	Great flow/zone, Totally sure
Focus on THE Best/compare/Extrinsic	1 2 3 4 5 6 7 8 9 10	Focus on MY Best/share/Intrinsic
Totally degraded others	1 2 3 4 5 6 7 8 9 10	Totally respected others
Totally belittled self	1 2 3 4 5 6 7 8 9 10	Totally respected self
Nada zip zero preparation/progress	1 2 3 4 5 6 7 8 9 10	Amazing preparation/progress
Total manipulation of others	1 2 3 4 5 6 7 8 9 10	No manipulation of others
Awful. Hated it. Grudges dragging	1 2 3 4 5 6 7 8 9 10	Great! Fun! No inner reservations. Flow/Zone

REFLECTIONS	Comments
Thoughts/feelings effecting output	
Possible cause of positive/negative changes	
Patterns or helpful observations	
Input from leader/mentor/friend	
Insights:	

Name _____ Cl _____

Core Power Pro-Launch Pad:
Propel Progress 4

Practice or performance (circle one)   **Date:**
TYPE of performance (circle) Tests/Sports/Business/Performing Arts/Other:
Observed problem/s:

Last goal completed? (circle) **Yes/No**
Type of Goal: (circle) Performance Ability/Emotional IQ/Life Balance/Respect self/Respect Others/No manipulation/Take Responsibility/Other:
Goal/s:

Observations	Notes
What happens	
When	
Where	
Why	
How Much	

CORE POWER PRO-LAUNCH PAD

OBSERVATIONS	Circle	Practice Performance (circle)
Worst ever quality	1 2 3 4 5 6 7 8 9 10	Awesome over-all quality
Incapacitating anxiety, Totally unsure	1 2 3 4 5 6 7 8 9 10	Great flow/zone, Totally sure
Focus on THE Best/compare/Extrinsic	1 2 3 4 5 6 7 8 9 10	Focus on MY Best/share/Intrinsic
Totally degraded others	1 2 3 4 5 6 7 8 9 10	Totally respected others
Totally belittled self	1 2 3 4 5 6 7 8 9 10	Totally respected self
Nada zip zero preparation/progress	1 2 3 4 5 6 7 8 9 10	Amazing preparation/progress
Total manipulation of others	1 2 3 4 5 6 7 8 9 10	No manipulation of others
Awful. Hated it. Grudges dragging	1 2 3 4 5 6 7 8 9 10	Great! Fun! No inner reservations. Flow/Zone

REFLECTIONS	Comments
Thoughts/feelings effecting output	
Possible cause of positive/negative changes	
Patterns or helpful observations	
Input from leader/mentor/friend	
Insights:	

Name _____ Cl _____

Core Power Pro-Launch Pad:
Propel Progress 5

Practice or performance (circle one)   **Date:**

TYPE of performance (circle) Tests/Sports/Business/Performing Arts/Other:

Observed problem/s:

Last goal completed? (circle) **Yes/No**

Type of Goal: (circle) Performance Ability/Emotional IQ/Life Balance/Respect self/Respect Others/No manipulation/Take Responsibility/Other:

Goal/s:

Observations	Notes
What happens	
When	
Where	
Why	
How Much	

OBSERVATIONS	Circle	Practice Performance (circle)
Worst ever quality	1 2 3 4 5 6 7 8 9 10	Awesome over-all quality
Incapacitating anxiety, Totally unsure	1 2 3 4 5 6 7 8 9 10	Great flow/zone, Totally sure
Focus on THE Best/compare/Extrinsic	1 2 3 4 5 6 7 8 9 10	Focus on MY Best/share/Intrinsic
Totally degraded others	1 2 3 4 5 6 7 8 9 10	Totally respected others
Totally belittled self	1 2 3 4 5 6 7 8 9 10	Totally respected self
Nada zip zero preparation/progress	1 2 3 4 5 6 7 8 9 10	Amazing preparation/progress
Total manipulation of others	1 2 3 4 5 6 7 8 9 10	No manipulation of others
Awful. Hated it. Grudges dragging	1 2 3 4 5 6 7 8 9 10	Great! Fun! No inner reservations. Flow/Zone

REFLECTIONS	Comments
Thoughts/feelings effecting output	
Possible cause of positive/negative changes	
Patterns or helpful observations	
Input from leader/mentor/friend	
Insights:	

Name _____ Cl _____

Core Power Pro-Launch Pad:
Propel Progress 6

Practice or performance (circle one)   **Date:**

TYPE of performance (circle) Tests/Sports/Business/Performing Arts/Other:

Observed problem/s:

Last goal completed? (circle) **Yes/No**

Type of Goal: (circle) Performance Ability/Emotional IQ/Life Balance/Respect self/Respect Others/No manipulation/Take Responsibility/Other:

Goal/s:

Observations	Notes
What happens	
When	
Where	
Why	
How Much	

OBSERVATIONS	Circle	Practice Performance (circle)
Worst ever quality	1 2 3 4 5 6 7 8 9 10	Awesome over-all quality
Incapacitating anxiety, Totally unsure	1 2 3 4 5 6 7 8 9 10	Great flow/zone, Totally sure
Focus on THE Best/compare/Extrinsic	1 2 3 4 5 6 7 8 9 10	Focus on MY Best/share/Intrinsic
Totally degraded others	1 2 3 4 5 6 7 8 9 10	Totally respected others
Totally belittled self	1 2 3 4 5 6 7 8 9 10	Totally respected self
Nada zip zero preparation/progress	1 2 3 4 5 6 7 8 9 10	Amazing preparation/progress
Total manipulation of others	1 2 3 4 5 6 7 8 9 10	No manipulation of others
Awful. Hated it. Grudges dragging	1 2 3 4 5 6 7 8 9 10	Great! Fun! No inner reservations. Flow/Zone

REFLECTIONS	Comments
Thoughts/feelings effecting output	
Possible cause of positive/negative changes	
Patterns or helpful observations	
Input from leader/mentor/friend	
Insights:	

Name _____ Cl _____

Core Power Pro-Launch Pad:
Propel Progress 7

Practice or performance (circle one)   **Date:**

TYPE of performance (circle) Tests/Sports/Business/Performing Arts/Other:

Observed problem/s:

Last goal completed? (circle) **Yes/No**

Type of Goal: (circle) Performance Ability/Emotional IQ/Life Balance/Respect self/Respect Others/No manipulation/Take Responsibility/Other:

Goal/s:

Observations	Notes
What happens	
When	
Where	
Why	
How Much	

OBSERVATIONS	Circle	Practice Performance (circle)
Worst ever quality	1 2 3 4 5 6 7 8 9 10	Awesome over-all quality
Incapacitating anxiety, Totally unsure	1 2 3 4 5 6 7 8 9 10	Great flow/zone, Totally sure
Focus on THE Best/compare/Extrinsic	1 2 3 4 5 6 7 8 9 10	Focus on MY Best/share/Intrinsic
Totally degraded others	1 2 3 4 5 6 7 8 9 10	Totally respected others
Totally belittled self	1 2 3 4 5 6 7 8 9 10	Totally respected self
Nada zip zero preparation/progress	1 2 3 4 5 6 7 8 9 10	Amazing preparation/progress
Total manipulation of others	1 2 3 4 5 6 7 8 9 10	No manipulation of others
Awful. Hated it. Grudges dragging	1 2 3 4 5 6 7 8 9 10	Great! Fun! No inner reservations. Flow/Zone

REFLECTIONS	Comments
Thoughts/feelings effecting output	
Possible cause of positive/negative changes	
Patterns or helpful observations	
Input from leader/mentor/friend	
Insights:	

Name _____ Cl _____

Core Power Pro-Launch Pad:
Propel Progress 8

Practice or performance (circle one)   **Date:**

TYPE of performance (circle) Tests/Sports/Business/Performing Arts/Other:

Observed problem/s:

Last goal completed? (circle) **Yes/No**

Type of Goal: (circle) Performance Ability/Emotional IQ/Life Balance/Respect self/Respect Others/No manipulation/Take Responsibility/Other:

Goal/s:

Observations	Notes
What happens	
When	
Where	
Why	
How Much	

OBSERVATIONS	Circle	Practice Performance (circle)
Worst ever quality	1 2 3 4 5 6 7 8 9 10	Awesome over-all quality
Incapacitating anxiety, Totally unsure	1 2 3 4 5 6 7 8 9 10	Great flow/zone, Totally sure
Focus on THE Best/compare/Extrinsic	1 2 3 4 5 6 7 8 9 10	Focus on MY Best/share/Intrinsic
Totally degraded others	1 2 3 4 5 6 7 8 9 10	Totally respected others
Totally belittled self	1 2 3 4 5 6 7 8 9 10	Totally respected self
Nada zip zero preparation/progress	1 2 3 4 5 6 7 8 9 10	Amazing preparation/progress
Total manipulation of others	1 2 3 4 5 6 7 8 9 10	No manipulation of others
Awful. Hated it. Grudges dragging	1 2 3 4 5 6 7 8 9 10	Great! Fun! No inner reservations. Flow/Zone

REFLECTIONS	Comments
Thoughts/feelings effecting output	
Possible cause of positive/negative changes	
Patterns or helpful observations	
Input from leader/mentor/friend	
Insights:	

Name _____ Cl _____

Core Power Pro-Launch Pad:
Propel Progress 9

Practice or performance (circle one)	**Date:**

TYPE of performance (circle) Tests/Sports/Business/Performing Arts/Other:

Observed problem/s:

Last goal completed? (circle) **Yes/No**

Type of Goal: (circle) Performance Ability/Emotional IQ/Life Balance/Respect self/Respect Others/No manipulation/Take Responsibility/Other:

Goal/s:

Observations	Notes
What happens	
When	
Where	
Why	
How Much	

OBSERVATIONS	Circle	Practice Performance (circle)
Worst ever quality	1 2 3 4 5 6 7 8 9 10	Awesome over-all quality
Incapacitating anxiety, Totally unsure	1 2 3 4 5 6 7 8 9 10	Great flow/zone, Totally sure
Focus on THE Best/compare/Extrinsic	1 2 3 4 5 6 7 8 9 10	Focus on MY Best/share/Intrinsic
Totally degraded others	1 2 3 4 5 6 7 8 9 10	Totally respected others
Totally belittled self	1 2 3 4 5 6 7 8 9 10	Totally respected self
Nada zip zero preparation/progress	1 2 3 4 5 6 7 8 9 10	Amazing preparation/progress
Total manipulation of others	1 2 3 4 5 6 7 8 9 10	No manipulation of others
Awful. Hated it. Grudges dragging	1 2 3 4 5 6 7 8 9 10	Great! Fun! No inner reservations. Flow/Zone

REFLECTIONS	Comments
Thoughts/feelings effecting output	
Possible cause of positive/negative changes	
Patterns or helpful observations	
Input from leader/mentor/friend	
Insights:	

Core Power Pro-Launch Pad:
Propel Progress 10

Practice or performance (circle one)   **Date:**

TYPE of performance (circle) Tests/Sports/Business/Performing Arts/Other:

Observed problem/s:

Last goal completed? (circle) **Yes/No**

Type of Goal: (circle) Performance Ability/Emotional IQ/Life Balance/Respect self/Respect Others/No manipulation/Take Responsibility/Other:

Goal/s:

Observations	Notes
What happens	
When	
Where	
Why	
How Much	

OBSERVATIONS	Circle	Practice Performance (circle)
Worst ever quality	1 2 3 4 5 6 7 8 9 10	Awesome over-all quality
Incapacitating anxiety, Totally unsure	1 2 3 4 5 6 7 8 9 10	Great flow/zone, Totally sure
Focus on THE Best/compare/Extrinsic	1 2 3 4 5 6 7 8 9 10	Focus on MY Best/share/Intrinsic
Totally degraded others	1 2 3 4 5 6 7 8 9 10	Totally respected others
Totally belittled self	1 2 3 4 5 6 7 8 9 10	Totally respected self
Nada zip zero preparation/progress	1 2 3 4 5 6 7 8 9 10	Amazing preparation/progress
Total manipulation of others	1 2 3 4 5 6 7 8 9 10	No manipulation of others
Awful. Hated it. Grudges dragging	1 2 3 4 5 6 7 8 9 10	Great! Fun! No inner reservations. Flow/Zone

REFLECTIONS	Comments
Thoughts/feelings effecting output	
Possible cause of positive/negative changes	
Patterns or helpful observations	
Input from leader/mentor/friend	
Insights:	

Name _____ Cl _____

Core Power Pro-Launch Pad:
Propel Progress 11

Practice or performance (circle one)   **Date:**

TYPE of performance (circle) Tests/Sports/Business/Performing Arts/Other:

Observed problem/s:

                                                           Last goal completed? (circle) **Yes/No**

Type of Goal: (circle) Performance Ability/Emotional IQ/Life Balance/Respect self/Respect Others/No manipulation/Take Responsibility/Other:

Goal/s:

Observations	Notes
What happens	
When	
Where	
Why	
How Much	

219

OBSERVATIONS	Circle	Practice Performance (circle)
Worst ever quality	1 2 3 4 5 6 7 8 9 10	Awesome over-all quality
Incapacitating anxiety, Totally unsure	1 2 3 4 5 6 7 8 9 10	Great flow/zone, Totally sure
Focus on THE Best/compare/Extrinsic	1 2 3 4 5 6 7 8 9 10	Focus on MY Best/share/Intrinsic
Totally degraded others	1 2 3 4 5 6 7 8 9 10	Totally respected others
Totally belittled self	1 2 3 4 5 6 7 8 9 10	Totally respected self
Nada zip zero preparation/progress	1 2 3 4 5 6 7 8 9 10	Amazing preparation/progress
Total manipulation of others	1 2 3 4 5 6 7 8 9 10	No manipulation of others
Awful. Hated it. Grudges dragging	1 2 3 4 5 6 7 8 9 10	Great! Fun! No inner reservations. Flow/Zone

REFLECTIONS	Comments
Thoughts/feelings effecting output	
Possible cause of positive/negative changes	
Patterns or helpful observations	
Input from leader/mentor/friend	
Insights:	

Name _____ Cl _____

Core Power Pro-Launch Pad:
Propel Progress 12

Practice or performance (circle one)   **Date:**

TYPE of performance (circle) Tests/Sports/Business/Performing Arts/Other:

Observed problem/s:

Last goal completed? (circle) **Yes/No**

Type of Goal: (circle) Performance Ability/Emotional IQ/Life Balance/Respect self/Respect Others/No manipulation/Take Responsibility/Other:

Goal/s:

Observations	Notes
What happens	
When	
Where	
Why	
How Much	

221

OBSERVATIONS	Circle	Practice Performance (circle)
Worst ever quality	1 2 3 4 5 6 7 8 9 10	Awesome over-all quality
Incapacitating anxiety, Totally unsure	1 2 3 4 5 6 7 8 9 10	Great flow/zone, Totally sure
Focus on THE Best/compare/Extrinsic	1 2 3 4 5 6 7 8 9 10	Focus on MY Best/share/Intrinsic
Totally degraded others	1 2 3 4 5 6 7 8 9 10	Totally respected others
Totally belittled self	1 2 3 4 5 6 7 8 9 10	Totally respected self
Nada zip zero preparation/progress	1 2 3 4 5 6 7 8 9 10	Amazing preparation/progress
Total manipulation of others	1 2 3 4 5 6 7 8 9 10	No manipulation of others
Awful. Hated it. Grudges dragging	1 2 3 4 5 6 7 8 9 10	Great! Fun! No inner reservations. Flow/Zone

REFLECTIONS	Comments
Thoughts/feelings effecting output	
Possible cause of positive/negative changes	
Patterns or helpful observations	
Input from leader/mentor/friend	
Insights:	

Name _____ Cl _____

Acknowledgements

My thanks to those I learned from and those who contributed ideas and support during the creation of *Boost Core Power and Bust Anxiety* and this companion workbook *The Core Power Pro-Launch Pad*. Compiling the information in these two companion books was a seven-year project which expanded from performance anxiety, to all educational anxieties, and finally to outcome anxiety. New insights and research were added in the process, adding to the breadth and depth. While the main acknowledgements are listed in the previous work, additional and significant persons in that process are acknowledged here: Dr. Bart Adams for his particular assistance and patience. James Adams, Michelle Adams, Sherie Christensen, Karen McNeff, Brian Adams, Julie Howald, Carolyn Richards, Ara Richards, James C. Richards, JaNae Richards, for their expertise, assistance and encouragement. Thanks also to Kamryn Brockbank for illustrations, and Teresa Lynn Anderson of Ann Lynn Photography. Thanks to my students for the things I learned from them.

Thanks also for support and feedback from Lynn Belnap, Dr. Linda Margetts, Christine Riesenweber, Ben Walley, Spring McGiffin, Associate Professor Bruce Walker, Michelle Maughan, Sarah Dodson, Mattie Lybbert, Pat Hagan, Chad Haertling, Matt Cooper, Claudia Wilson, Crystal Field, Chanda Hunt, Ann Perry, Dawn Goodrich, Kathryn Burton, Tiah Peterson, Dylan Clemons, Patty Case, Melinda Gill, Jenna Lake, Jennifer Buckner, Jeanie Lemens, Hayley Lemens, The Honorable Gordon Smith, Sharon Smith, Kenny Steward, Evan Lake, Eadie Jordan, Dennis Waite, Penni Waite, Maxine Patterson, Cherish Lloyd , Cody Fielding, Diane Bricker, Deanna Lambson, Garnet Olsen, Lily Ann Gwillam, Dr. Sushma Hirani, Vanessa Orellana, Dr. Sharlene Milner, Jasleen Orellana, Trent Christensen, Em Adams, Mathew McNeff, and Carl Howald, V, Lee Richards, Mark David Richards, Brett Gerlach, Diane Whitehead, Donald Cook, Holly Harty, Marsha Carter.

Special thanks also to the Oregon Music Teachers Association; NYC FD support, cooperation, and commendation; BYU International Organ Workshop; Brigham Young University, particularly the dance, music, theater, and education departments; RG Studios; LA East Studios; Dance Educators of America; Utah Department of Education; Blue Mountain Community College, particularly the music and theater departments; Oregon East Symphony; Columbia Basin Community College, particularly the psychology and music departments; the University of Utah, particularly the dance, music and theater departments; American Mothers, Inc.; Eastern Oregon University, particularly the education and music departments; USA military support for NOK; the Washington Music Teachers Association; Oregon Department of Education; California Southern University, particularly the psychology department and library research; and the Music Teachers National Association.

About the Author

Mariann Richards Adams is an internationally featured anxiety expert with experience in radio and TV. She is the author of two books and numerous articles. She presents lectures for professional organizations, universities, conferences, and businesses, as well as providing private anxiety coaching and teaching. Her masters degree was from Eastern Oregon University in music, theater, dance (PE) education, specializing in educational and performance anxieties. Her PhD studies are currently at California Southern University in clinical psychology, specializing in anxiety. Her first teaching was as an assistant to Stephen R. Covey. She now has decades of experience as a teacher, choreographer, musician, and theater director; has performed in the majority of states in the USA; and was a member of the acclaimed Young Ambassadors. She wrote and directed a celebration in Old Town San Diego for the LA Olympics, and a historical play for the Mayo Clinic centennial celebrations. A CD that her family created has been distributed throughout the United States to the families of fallen US military. She created a multi-specialty surgery center, two non-profits, and A+ Performing Arts. She is the recipient of the Oregon Mother of Achievement, NYC FD Commendation, and the BYU Alumni Distinguished Service Award. Her greatest joy is as a wife and mother to her wonderful children and delightful grandchildren. She loves to bicycle along the Columbia River and paddle board.

www.ingramcontent.com/pod-product-compliance
Lightning Source LLC
Chambersburg PA
CBHW081947070426
42453CB00013BA/2274